© Naumann & Göbel Verlagsgesellschaft mbH, a subsidiary of
VEMAG Verlags- und Medien Aktiengesellschaft, Cologne
www.apollo-intermedia.de

Complete production: Naumann & Göbel Verlagsgesellschaft mbH, Cologne
Printed in Poland

ISBN 3-625-11132-2

Barbecuing

NAUMANN & GÖBEL

FOREWORD

Barbecuing is not just fun during the summer. Thanks to modern technology, this romantic campfire atmosphere can be extended over the whole year. Whether charcoal fire or electric grill, this form of cooking is very healthy. Due to the intensive heat radiation, the pores of the grilled meat close quickly, which means, that it becomes crispy on the outside and soft and juicy on the inside in a short time. You can grill almost everything: meat, fish, poultry, game, vegetables, fruit, mushrooms, etc. You can always get new flavours with marinades, spices and other refinements. With a little creativity you can also make small culinary works of art from simple, cheap ingredients.

So enjoy!

CONTENTS

In the beginning, there were only meat and fire...

The origin of fire itself is as mysterious to mankind as the flickering of burning flames.

In ancient Greece, Prometheus is thought to have lit a dry reed on the sun god's carriage. Other cultures considered it as a sign and gift of the gods, because it fell directly from the sky as lightning. But no matter, how and where it came from, the practical use of fire was very quickly discovered – for heating and cooking. At first, cooking was done outside over an open fire. War and hunting equipment such as lances, spears, swords and knives were useful for skewering meat and holding it over the fire. Evolution taught men how to build houses, and they also "civilised" their heating and cooking places. The barbarous campfire became a peaceful hearth. Then in modern times large technical changes came into the kitchen. Electricity and gas simplified cooking and heating. Everything became more comfortable. The daily ration of meat did not have to be hunted dangerously any more. The fire also was suddenly tame and the view to the sky was walled off. Now, one wants to go back to freedom, campfire and adventure.

This is probably one explanation for the increasing enthusiasm for cooking and eating outdoors, and the interesting social and culinary culture that has developed around the barbecue.

Herbs and Spices

First, all herbs and spices should refine the taste of meals, but their importance to health can also not be neglected. In the correct quantities, they improve the digestion of a meal. Moreover, they help to save salt, which is very important for healthy nutrition. According to medical knowledge, an adult man does not need more than 5 g (0.2 oz) of salt per day. To provide the body with the necessary iodine, you should only use iodine salt or coarse sea salt. (Lack of iodine leads to abnormal changes in the thyroid.)

Herbs are tender small plants. Every one of them has its own special aroma and taste. The aroma is more intensive, as the proportion of essential oils increases. Some herbs must not be cooked, as they lose their strength or become bitter when heated for a long time.

Herbs with fine leaves such as basil, borage, tarragon, dill, chervil, parsley, pimpernel, chives and lemon balm are not added to the meals until just before serving them. Strong herbs such as marjoram, savory, lovage, mugwort, sage, thyme and rosemary can be cooked for longer times. Fresh herbs should not be cut until immediately before using them, preferably on a plastic or marble cutting board. Wooden boards are not so well-suited as they suck up the juice too fast and are also difficult to clean. It is recommended to grow fresh herbs yourself so that you always have access to them. As they only require flower soil, some heat and water, they can be grown easily near the kitchen window or on the balcony. Everything you do not use immediately can be stored. With only a few exceptions, all herbs can be frozen. We always freeze them as whole sprigs in a bundle, because they can be crumbled easily when frozen. You can also chop them coarsely and freeze them in portions (also as a mixture). Marjoram, thyme, savory, mugwort, sage and rosemary are hung in a well-aired space to dry. If you do not have enough room, you can "quick dry" them in the oven (max. 50 °C/122 °F). Afterwards they are crumbled coarsely and stored. Herb oil and herb vinegar can be homemade easily. Especially for barbecueing, they then have a very individual taste. And while you are making things: they make a nice present for various occasions when filled in unusual bottles. Dried herbs (either as whole sprigs or crushed coarsely) are used for making a herb oil. For herb vinegars, fresh herbs are used, usually as a whole sprig to make it look very decorative in a nice bottle. While the oil needs a good 6 – 8 weeks to get its right taste, the herb vinegar is ready in 1 – 2 weeks. Herb vinegar can be stored for 1 – 2 years in a dark place. In contrast, even for proper storage, herb oils should be used within 6 – 8 weeks.

Freshly chopped or finely ground herbs and spices are mixed with some oil for a spice paste.

Liquid marinades with a lot of oil are ideal to prevent lean grill meat from drying out during cooking.

The use of fresh herbs is recommended for most of the following recipes. You can of course also use dried herbs. 1 tablespoon of dried herbs is the equivalent of one sprig of fresh herbs. Dried herbs become more aromatic and soft, when they are put into an oil-bath for 10–15 minutes before being used. The table shows you which herbs and spices are suitable for which meals.

Depending on their ingredients, marinades can be mild or spicy, dry or liquid, sweet or sour and give the barbecue a certain flavour. Dry marinades are a mixture of dry herbs (which are ground in a mortar), spices and salt.

Sour marinades, based on wine, vinegar or lemon juice, make grilled meat especially tender and mellow.

Used with:	basil	savory	curry	dill	tarragon	ginger	chervil	garlic	sage	chives	thyme	onion
meat	●		●		●	●		●	●	●	●	●
fish			●	●	●		●	●				●
game					●				●		●	●
mince	●		●			●		●				
sauces	●	●	●	●	●	●	●	●	●	●		
potatoes				●				●		●	●	●
poultry	●		●					●		●	●	●
vegetables	●	●		●	●			●	●			●

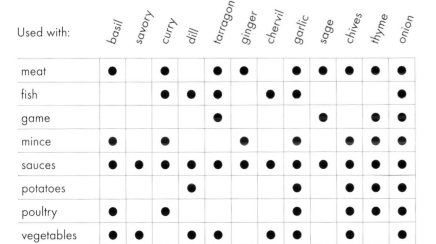

Meat can be marinated for up to 48 hours in the fridge. For fish and shellfish, 2–3 hours is usually enough.

Grilling tips

Parties outside are always a wonderfully thrilling pleasure. The origin of the names picnic and barbecue is not known exactly.

"Picnic" probably comes from French and does not mean anything other than "eating outside".
Of course, the ordinary people did not create this fashionable phenomenon. It was the aristocracy who celebrated feasts with lots of imagination and even more money. You can also celebrate feasts with us. We have prepared a lot of fun ideas for you – from the children's picnic to the large American barbecue.
The word "barbecue" comes from "barbacias", which is what the native inhabitants of middle America and the Caribbean called their cooking pits covered with green wood. A simple, but very effective cooking method. The colonists obviously shared this opinion, because they went on to develop the worldwide famous and beloved barbecue.
For the following suggestions, we have assumed that your picnic or barbecue will be set up under a tent or a similar type of construction. First, the menu sequence can be adapted as required depending on the theme of your party and/or on the mood of your guests at the time, and secondly smart side dishes and decorations add something special to the dishes.
You also have a lot of options for your own creativity.
Whether it is a large or a small party, there is one thing we cannot do for you – the planning. Based on

the maxim "Good organisation is just as important as nice guests", we have developed a short checklist which can be expanded or reduced as needed.

1. Occasion
Casual, informal, specific event etc.

2. Number of people

3. Menu and drinks
Especially important: What can be prepared before hand, or bought already finished? What and how will certain dishes be prepared during the event? Calculate the servings generously, as they taste especially delicious outdoors.

4. Means of transport

5. Transport containers
Packing, cooling, keeping warm

6. Plates and cutlery
Cardboard, china, metal, plastic etc ...

7. Decorations

8. Bread, rolls, nibbles

9. Grill appliance, charcoal

10. Rubbish bags

Suckling pig preparation
There is also a suggestion for a suckling pig meal in our picnic and barbecue ideas section. We show you step by step how the animal is fixed onto the spit and carved up afterwards. It is not difficult at all, and a real "barbecuer" must try it at least once in his life.

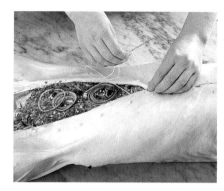

Stuffing and sewing up
The kitchen-ready suckling pig prepared by the butcher is rinsed inside and outside, rubbed dry and then placed on a worktop. The stuffing is flattened into the well spiced inside of the belly. Afterwards the animal is sewn up with strong kitchen twine. Be careful to make the stitches approx. 1.5 – 2 cm (0.6 – 0.8 in) away from the edge so that the suture does not rip open during grilling.

Placing onto the spit
Putting the suckling pig onto the spit is very easy when you lay the animal on its side, hold its hind paws firmly with one hand and push the skewer with gentle pressure up to its snout. The spit should protrude a good 30 – 40 cm (12 – 15 in) at both ends so that the animal is lying on it well-balanced and securely.

Fixing securely

In order to prevent your suckling pig from falling into the ashes, it should be fixed on the spit in three places. First, at the buttocks: for this you use the adjustable spit joint holder and screw it firmly in place when it is pushed right up to the meat.

Browning evenly

With a complete animal on a spit, it happens very easily that some parts cook faster than others do. The ears and trotters should be covered with aluminium foil to prevent them from burning. Furthermore, for this relatively long grilling process, you have to regularly replenish the charcoal to keep the temperature constant.

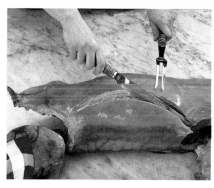

Separating the chops

When this is done, it is time for the chops. The string of chops is cut off in one piece. This piece is obtained by cutting into the back down to the bone and pulling the knife downwards along the ribs. Afterwards the meat is cut up into portions.

Binding the front and hind feet

Then, the front and hind feet are bound together with a flexible, non-rusting wire. Both feet are first wrapped up with wire separately and afterwards both loose ends of the wire are twisted together to bring the feet together so that the weight of the animal is better distributed. Be careful to leave the ends of the wire long enough (approx. 20–30 cm (8–12 in)) for binding the pig to the spit.

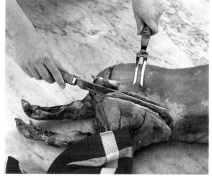

Carving the suckling pig

After the grilling is finished, the work really starts. The suckling pig must be carved up properly. You need a sufficiently large working space and a sharp carving knife and fork for this. First, the ham is cut off, the back ham with one strong cut from the hip to the tail, the shoulder ham also with a strong cut from the shoulderblade to the ear.

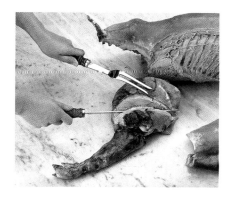

Separating the upper and lower legs

The upper and lower legs are always cut through at the joint. For all carving processes, the fork is used to hold the meat firmly. Do not stab into the meat, instead only press the joint firmly onto the work surface. If you stab into the meat, too much of the delicious meat juices will flow out.

Gutting and preparing fish for grilling

Belly side up, cut open the fish with a sharp, pointed knife from its back opening up to the throat (photo 1). Then there are four steps: first, remove the offal (photo 2); second, wash the fish thoroughly (photo 3); third, carve several slits on both sides of the fish and put fresh herbs into the slits; and, fourth, clamp the fish into the grill basket (photo 4).

Preparing a chicken for grilling

Method without a needle:
Place the kitchen twine underneath the back. Cross the twine over the belly opening and wrap around the lower legs behind the drumsticks (photo 5). Pull the twine up over the wings, wrap around the wings, turn the chicken over and knot the twine (photo 6).

Method with a needle:
Stuff the chicken and sew up the opening (photo 7). Put the needle through the wings and sew the skin of the neck to the backbone (photo 8). Turn the chicken over and fix the legs to the body (photo 9). Lay the chicken on its side and knot both ends of the twine (photo 10). Turn the tips of the wings inwards and sew up through the wingtips and skin (photo 11). Fix the lower legs in the same way (photo 12).

photo 1

photo 2

photo 3

photo 4

photo 5

photo 6

photo 7

photo 8

photo 9

photo 10

photo 11

photo 12

Separating poultry into portions

Push the legs apart and cut into the skin. Disconnect the joint and cut through with a knife (photo 13). Cut through the legs at the joint (photo 14). Cut between the breast and the wing joint to detach the wing (photo 15). Then push the knife through the flesh and cut along the sides of the ribcage (photo 16). Pull the breast fillet away from the ribcage and cut it off (photo 17). Cut in this manner on both sides and separate the two sections (photo 18).

Preparing veal kidneys for grilling

Cut the kidneys into two pieces (photo 19) and cut out the fat and sinews with a sharp knife (photo 20).

Larding a roast and fixing it in the grill basket.

Cut a fatty bacon into long strips (photo 21) and fix the strips in a larding needle (photo 22). Pull the needle through the piece of meat (photo 23). Fix the finished roast in the grill basket (photo 24).

photo 13

photo 14

photo 15

photo 16

photo 17

photo 18

photo 19

photo 20

photo 21

photo 22

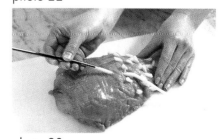

photo 23

photo 24

Preparing rolled roasts

Roll the meat up tightly.

When the end of the joint is reached, the whole thing is turned over. The twine is pulled through the crossing threads lengthways.

Tie a knot around one end of the roast with some strong kitchen twine.

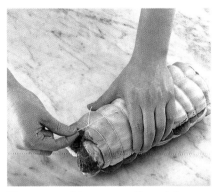

Knot everything up well and the perfect rolled roast is ready.

Depending on the size of the roast, wrap the twine around the roll in intervals 2–3 cm (0.8–1.2 in) distance from one another. Always putting the twine through the thread that is situated lengthways.

Wrapping grillades in bacon

Lean grillades love a made-to-measure coat of bacon to stay juicy.

For this, finely cut slices of fresh or smoked bacon are wrapped around the spiced meat and tied in place with kitchen twine.

Grilling steaks

It is not a difficult art to grill a steak properly if you have a well aged piece of meat. It must be brown and crispy on the outside and, depending on your taste, bloody to well-done on the inside.

With a little experience, you can establish the best cooking point with the thumb test. The more elastic the meat feels the more raw it is.

A steak of 200 g (7 oz) and a thickness of 2 cm (0.8 in) is described as follows by the gourmet:

- 1 minute grilling time per side: Blue. The meat has a thin strong crust, but the rest is raw.

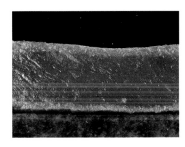

blue

- A good 2 minutes grilling time per side: Rare. The meat has a somewhat thicker strong crust and a raw centre with a pink colour.

rare

- A good 3 minutes grilling time per side: Medium rare. The meat has a thicker strong crust and is cooked through up to a good finger's thickness with pink strips. The meat juices are still red.

medium rare

- A good 4 minutes grilling time per side: Medium. The meat is cooked through up to a narrow pink-coloured strip.

medium

- A good 5 minutes grilling time per side: Well done. Steaks should not be cooked any longer, as the meat can easily become tough.

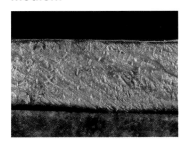

well done

A meat thermometer can be very helpful for larger pieces of meat. It is put into the meat before grilling (not into the fat or near a bone). Depending on the kind of meat, it is well-done at 75–85 °C/167–185 °F. At about 60 °C/140 °F it is pink on the inside. While lamb and beef can be served at different degrees of cooking, pork and veal should always be well-done.
After grilling, larger pieces of meat should be left to settle for a while so that they become hard and do not lose their juices. They are always cut across the grain of the meat.
Charcoal is used predominantly for grilling outdoors. Simple coal is quicker to light, but it does not glow as long. Charcoal briquettes are more solid and thus glow longer. Commercially available fire-lighters mixed in with the briquettes make igniting them easier. It is dangerous to use petrol or other similar inflammable liquids as "quick lighters". Furthermore, children should always keep a safe distance away from the fire.

The barbecue site outside should be chosen carefully and not near woodsheds, bales of straw, dry bushes etc. If you are grilling while travelling, keep to signposted grill or picnic places. Grillades get a special aroma when you burn the wood from fruit trees or herb branches. Pine cones make a special treat of thin pork sausages.
The grilling can start when a white coating of ash has formed on the charcoal or briquettes. You should take care that the coals lie close to each other to guarantee the optimum generation of heat. The aluminium grill trays available in the shops are practical. They have grooves and slots that let the charcoal aroma through while preventing fat and liquid falling into the fire at the same time.

Toast and Snacks

Delicious things prepared quickly and in a refined way. Creative ideas for the whole year, which you can change according to your taste and mood.

TROUT TOAST

Serves 4

4 slices of toast
bread

butter for spreading

6 tbsp
of mayonnaise

3 tbsp cream

1 tsp chopped capers

2 tsp grated
horseradish

150 g (5 oz) smoked
fillet of trout

salt, pepper

1 onion

4 slices of Gouda
cheese

1 tbsp trout caviar

parsley for garnishing

Preparation time:
20 minutes
Cooking time:
10 minutes

Per serving:
approx. 2273 kJ / 544 cal
18 g protein, 43 g fat,
21 g carbohydrate

1 Slightly toast the bread and spread
with butter.

2 Mix the mayonnaise with the cream.
Add the capers and horseradish. Tear
the trout fillet into pieces and add it to the
mixture. Spice with salt and pepper.

3 Peel and dice the onion. Spread the
trout mixture onto the bread, sprinkle
the cubes of onion over it and cover with
the slices of cheese.

4 Grill the trout toast in an electric grill
for about 5 minutes. Serve garnished
with caviar and parsley.

CHILI MEATBALLS

1 Spice the minced meat with the coriander powder, salt, pepper and sugar. Knead the egg and the cornflour with the minced meat.

2 Pour boiling water over the Mu err (Chinese Morel) mushrooms and let them soften in it for about 10 minutes.

3 Cut the chili in half, wash it and dice.

4 Peel the cloves of garlic and press them. Strain the liquid from the bamboo shoots, shake off the excess liquid and cut them into fine pieces.

5 Strain the liquid from the mushrooms, press them dry and cut them into fine strips. Knead the prepared ingredients with the minced meat and shape it into small balls.

6 Put the chili meatballs onto skewers and grill them on the barbecue for 12 minutes until they are brown and cooked on every side.

7 Arrange the chili meatballs on the chili sauce, garnish and serve.

Serves 4

500 g (17 oz) mixed minced meat

2 tsp coriander powder

salt, pepper

sugar

1 egg

1 tbsp cornflour

3 dried Mu-err (Chinese Morel) mushrooms

1 red chili

2 cloves of garlic

150 g (5 oz) canned bamboo shoots

1 bottle of chili sauce

Preparation time:
30 minutes
Cooking time:
15 minutes

Per serving:
approx. 1803 kJ /431 cal
29 g protein, 23 g fat,
20 g carbohydrates

MINCED TURKEY LIVERS IN PLUM SAUCE

Serves 4

10 lychees

300 g (10.6 oz) turkey liver

2 tsp Chinese mixed-spices

2 tbsp Hoisin sauce

1 tbsp oil

150 g (5 oz) streaky bacon

8 slices of toast bread

2 cm (0.8in) ginger root

3 tbsp Asian plum sauce (ready made)

4 tbsp lemon juice

pepper

mint for garnishing

Preparation time
(without marinating time):
30 minutes
Cooking time:
25 minutes

Per serving
approx. 2424 kJ / 580 cal
24 g protein, 33 g fat,
41 g carbohydrates

1 Peel the lychees and remove the stones. Wash the turkey liver, dry it and put it in a bowl.

2 Mix the spice powder with the Peking sauce and pour it over the liver. Marinate the liver for about 30 minutes.

3 Then shake off the excess liquid from the liver and fry it in the oil on both sides.

4 Add the lychees and fry everything together for about 10 minutes. Then combine both into a fine puree.

5 Cut the bacon into slices. Cut the slices of bread into quarters, toast them and spread the liver purée on top of them. Wrap with bacon and grill all of them until they are crisp and brown.

6 Peel and chop the ginger finely. Spice the plum sauce with the ginger, lemon juice and pepper and arrange the pieces of liver on it. Garnish with the mint and serve.

GRILLED SCALLOPS

1 Place the scallops in a colander and let them thaw. Rinse afterwards and dab dry.

2 Mix the soy sauce with the fish sauce, sherry, salt, sugar and the vegetables in a saucepan and bring to the boil.

3 Quickly dip the scallops in the sauce, shake off the excess liquid and put them onto the skewer.

4 Place the skewer on the grill for about 5 minutes turning the skewer frequently.

5 Let the sauce boil down a little and serve it hot onto the scallops. Serve the complete dish garnished with watercress.

Serves 4

500 g (17 oz) frozen scallops

60 ml (2 fl oz) soy sauce

1 tbsp fish sauce

60 ml (2 fl oz) cream sherry

1 tsp salt

1 tsp sugar

100 g (3.5 oz) finely cut, mixed vegetables (carrots, celery, leek)

watercress for garnishing

Preparation time (without thawing time): 20 minutes
Cooking time: 10 minutes

Per serving
approx. 609 kJ /145 cal
15 g protein, 1 g fat,
11 g carbohydrates

PEPPERED PRAWNS

Serves 4

12 king prawns with shell

125 ml (4 fl oz) soy sauce

4 tbsp sherry

1 tsp pepper

4 spring onions

1 tbsp oil

3 tbsp tomato ketchup

1 tbsp cornflour

4 tbsp rice wine

herbs for garnishing

Preparation time (without marinating time): 25 minutes
Cooking time: 15 minutes

Per serving approx. 724 kJ / 172 cal 13 g protein, 4 g fat, 10 g carbohydrates

1 Remove the tail of the prawn with a quarter turn of its head. Grab the shell from underneath with both hands and pull it apart. Remove the dark intestine on the rear side with a knife.

2 Stir 3 tbsp of the soy sauce with the sherry and the pepper. Add the prawns and let them marinate for 30 minutes.

3 Wash the spring onions and cut them into quarters. Take the prawns out of the marinade and put them onto the skewer with spring onions in between each. Brush with oil and grill for 10 minutes while turning frequently.

4 Mix the ketchup with the rest of the soy sauce, the cornflour and the rice wine. Pour into a saucepan, let it boil, and serve it as a sauce with the prawns. Garnish the whole dish with herbs.

SPICY CHEESE ON TOAST

1 Toast the bread and spread with butter.

2 Grill the bacon slices for about 2 minutes and have them ready.

3 Press the blue cheese with a fork and mix it with the pear spirit and some pepper. Then spread it onto the toast bread.

4 First lay the bacon slices onto the cheese mixture, then the Gouda slices. Grill the cheese toasts for about 5 minutes and serve them garnished with parsley.

Serves 4

4 slices of three corn multi-grain toast bread

butter for spreading

4 slices of streaky bacon

200 g (7 oz) of blue cheese

2 cl (scant 1 fl oz) of pear spirit

fresh ground pepper

4 slices of Gouda cheese

parsley for garnishing

Preparation time:
10 minutes
Cooking time:
7 minutes

Per serving
approx. 2221 kJ / 531 cal
23 g protein, 41 g fat,
16 g carbohydrates

HERB BURGER

Serves 4

2 gherkins

2 bundles of mixed herbs

500 g (17 oz) mixed minced meat

salt

pepper

paprika powder

2 eggs

2 tbsp bread crumbs

4 hamburger buns

100 g (3.5 oz) herb butter

4 lettuce leaves

4 tbsp tomato ketchup

Preparation time: 25 minutes
Cooking time: 15 minutes

Per serving approx. 2580 kJ / 617 cal 34 g protein, 37 g fat, 34 g carbohydrates

1 Cut the gherkins into small cubes. Wash the herbs, dry them and chop them finely.

2 Mix the minced meat with the herbs, the gherkins, salt, pepper, and paprika powder.

3 Knead the meat paste with the eggs and the breadcrumbs. Using wet hands, make four burgers out of the paste.

4 Grill the burgers on the grill for about 6 minutes on each side.

5 Cut the hamburger buns in half and toast them on the grill for a short time until they are a golden yellow colour. Afterwards spread herb butter on to the bottom halves of the buns.

6 Place a lettuce leaf and a burger on each bottom half of the buns. Cover the burger with ketchup and then cover with the top half of the bun. Serve immediately.

Tip

If you like the herb burger especially spicy, spread the bun halves with pepper or garlic butter and use stronger spicy ketchup.

CHEESEBURGER

Cut 100 g (3.5 oz) of Gouda cheese into small cubes, knead with 500 g (17 oz) of mixed minced meat, 1 cubed onion, 1 egg, 2 tbsp of breadcrumbs, salt, pepper and paprika powder. Make four burgers out of this and cook on the grill for about 6 minutes on each side. Cut 4 hamburger buns in half and toast them. Then place 1 lettuce leaf, 1 burger, some of the tomato slices and 1 slice of cheese on the bottom halves of the buns. Cover with the upper halves of the buns and serve immediately.

Serves 4

Preparation time:
25 minutes
Cooking time:
15 minutes

Per serving
approx. 1995 kJ / 477 cal
39 g protein, 22 g fat,
32 g carbohydrate

CHILIBURGER

Mix 1 bunch of finely chopped spring onions the chopped chili, 500 g (17 oz) of minced beef, salt, paprika powder, 2 eggs and 2 tbsp of breadcrumbs. Make 4 burgers out of this mixture and cook them on the grill for about 6 minutes on each side. Cut 4 hamburger buns in half and place slices of cucumber on the bottom halves followed by the hamburgers. Spice with chili ketchup, and then lay 2 rings of onions on top and cover with the upper half of the bun.

Serves 4

Preparation time:
20 minutes
Cooking time:
15 minutes

Per serving
approx. 1881 kJ / 448 cal
32 g protein, 15 g fat,
40 g carbohydrates

CHEESE AND PAPRIKA SAUSAGES

Serves 4

8 bockwurst sausages

100 g (3.5 oz) soft cheese

paprika powder

120 g (4.2 oz) bacon

Preparation time:
15 minutes
Cooking time:
10 minutes

Per serving
approx. 2662 kJ / 634 cal
35 g protein, 50 g fat,
0,8 g carbohydrates

1 Slice the sausages open lengthways so that they can be folded open. Do not cut them completely in half.

2 First, cut the cheese into long strips. Place the strips of cheese inside the sausages and sprinkle them with paprika powder.

3 Close the sausages and wrap them with bacon.

4 Grill the cheese and paprika sausages on the grill for about 5 minutes on each side.

Tip

If you like the sausages to be spicier, use hot paprika powder. Or mix mild paprika powder with some chili powder and hot mustard. Spread the paste on the inside of the sausages and cover it with the strips of cheese.

SARDINES ON TOAST

1 Toast the slices of bread and spread them with butter

2 Finely grate the cheese and combine in a double boiler with the beer, mustard, Worcestershire sauce, cornflour and the pepper until it is the consistency of cream.

3 Spread the cream onto the slices of bread and grill on the electric grill for 5 minutes.

4 Shake the excess liquid off the sardines and lay them on the slices of bread and garnish with sprigs of dill

Serves 4

4 slices of wholemeal toast bread

butter for spreading

250 g (9 oz) old Gouda cheese

6 tbsp dark beer

1 tbsp mustard

Worcestershire sauce

1 tbsp cornflour

pepper

1 can of sardines in oil without skin and backbone (150 g/5 oz)

sprigs of dill for garnishing

Preparation time:
20 minutes
Cooking time:
5 minutes

Per serving:
approx. 1772 kJ / 424 cal
28 g protein, 28 g fat,
14 g carbohydrates

TOAST "PROVENCE"

Serves 4

4 tomatoes

1 onion

1 clove of garlic

2 tbsp oil

2 tsp herbes de Provence

salt

pepper

4 slices of rye bread

butter for spreading

6 slices of Emmental cheese

3 hardboiled eggs

4 bockwurst sausages

herbs for garnishing

Preparation time:
30 minutes
Cooking time:
10 minutes

Per serving
approx. 3243 kJ / 776 cal
35 g protein, 58 g fat,
24 g carbohydrates

1 Cut a cross in the tomatoes, pour boiling water over them, peel, remove the seeds and cut into cubes.

2 Peel and dice the onion and the clove of garlic. Heat the oil and lightly sauté the onions with the garlic. Add the diced tomato and fry for 5 minutes. Spice the sauce with the herbs, salt and pepper and let it simmer for about 1 minute.

3 Toast the slices of bread and spread them with butter. Pour the sauce over them.

4 Put a slice of cheese on each slice of bread. Peel the eggs, cut them into slices and put them on the cheese.

5 Cut the bockwurst sausages in half lengthways and lay them on top of the slices of egg.

6 Cut the rest of the cheese into slices and put them in crosses over the bockwurst sausages. Grill the whole dish for 5 minutes in the electric grill and serve garnished with herbs.

SAUSAGE ROLL

1 Mix together the mustard, ketchup, the white wine, and the pepper.

2 Peel and core the apple, then slice.

3 Roll the sausage into the shape of a large snail.

4 Cut the bacon into pieces, then intersperse it with the slices of onion and apple in the rolled sausage.

5 Put about 8 skewers in the sausage roll to keep it in shape and cook it on the grill for about 10 minutes on each side. Baste with the prepared sauce while cooking.

Serves 4

2 tbsp Dijon mustard

2 tbsp tomato ketchup

2 tbsp white wine

2 tbsp Maggi

Cayenne pepper

1 apple

1 onion

700 g (1 lb 8 oz) uncooked frying sausage in pieces

4 slices of breakfast bacon

Preparation time: 20 minutes
Cooking time: 20 minutes

Per serving approx. 2887 kJ / 691 cal 35 g protein, 54 g fat, 7 g carbohydrates

SAUSAGE SKEWERS

Serves 4

1 red pepper

1 yellow pepper

3 spring onions

150 g (5 oz) streaky bacon

24 sausages

2 tbsp oil

1/2 tsp paprika powder

salt

pepper

1 tsp mixed, chopped herbs

Preparation time:
20 minutes
Cooking time:
15 minutes

Per serving
approx. 2572 kJ / 615 cal
23 g protein, 49 g fat,
7 g carbohydrates

1 Wash the peppers and cut into large pieces. Clean the spring onions, and cut them into quarters.

2 First cut the bacon into thick slices and then into chunks.

3 Next, place the sausages, the paprika, onion and bacon pieces onto the skewers.

4 Mix the oil with the spices and the herbs, brush the skewers with this mixture and grill for about 15 minutes turning frequently.

KIWI BURGER

1 Peel and dice the onion. Crumble the roll into a fine texture and add it, together with the diced onion, to the minced meat.

2 Add the egg mixed with the spices and mustard to the minced meat. Knead the ingredients carefully to make a meat dough.

3 Peel the kiwi and cut it into slices. With wet hands, make 4 burgers out of the minced meat. Place a slice of kiwi on each side of the burger and press firmly into the dough.

4 Brush the burgers with oil and cook on the grill for about 6 minutes on each side.

Serves 4

1 onion

1 day old roll

500 g (17 oz) mixed minced meat

1 egg

salt

pepper

paprika powder

1 pinch of mustard

1 tsp steak spice mixture

1 kiwi

oil for brushing

Preparation time:
20 minutes
Cooking time:
15 minutes

Per serving
approx. 1291 kJ / 309 cal
28 g protein, 17 g fat,
9 g carbohydrates

41

TURKISH LAMB SKEWERS

Serves 4

500 g (17 oz) lamb meat from the haunch/loin

2 cloves of garlic

1 onion

1 red pepper

1 soft roll

1 egg

salt

1 pinch chili powder

paprika powder

2 cups of yoghurt

1 tbsp chopped, mixed herbs

Preparation time:
35 minutes
Cooking time:
20 minutes

Per serving
approx. 1918 kJ / 456 cal
11 g protein, 27 g fat,
12 g carbohydrates

1 Wash and dry the lamb meat and then cut it into large cubes.

2 Peel the cloves of garlic and the onion. Chop the onion coarsely.

3 Cut the pepper in half, remove the seeds, place it on a baking tray with the skin side up and bake it in a preheated oven at 250 °C/482 °F for about 15 minutes. Let it cool down afterwards and carefully remove the skin.

4 Mince the lamb meat together with one clove of garlic, the onion, the red pepper and the roll.

5 Mix the meat mixture with the egg and the spices, shape into 8 rolls and place them lengthways on skewers. Grill for about 12 minutes with frequent turning.

6 For the sauce, press the rest of the garlic together with salt and mix with the yoghurt. Then add the herbs. Spice the garlic sauce with salt and serve with the skewers.

BURGER WITH FRIED EGG (SUNNY SIDE UP)

1 Spice the minced meat with salt, pepper and the mixed spices. Knead one egg and the roll into the minced meat.

2 Make 4 burgers out of the mixture and cook them on the grill for about 6 minutes on each side and keep them warm.

3 Place the slices of bread on the grill and toast them for a short time.

4 Peel the clove of garlic and cut it in half and rub it into the slices of bread.

5 First place a lettuce leaf and then one burger onto each slice of bread. Pour tomato ketchup over this.

6 Fry the remaining eggs sunny side up. Place these onto the burgers and serve immediately.

Tip
Have a look at the skin colouring between the cloves of garlic. If this is a light pink colour, then it is really fresh.

Serves 4

500 g (17 oz) beef mince

salt

pepper

mixed spices for minced meat (onion, garlic, marjoram, nutmeg, caraway)

5 eggs

1 soft roll

4 slices of farmhouse bread

1 clove of garlic

4 lettuce leaves

4 tbsp tomato ketchup

butter for frying

Preparation time: 15 minutes
Cooking time: 20 minutes

Per serving approx. 2107 kJ / 501 cal 31 g protein, 22 g fat, 34 g carbohydrates

STUFFED MUSHROOMS

Serves 4

500 g (17 oz) fresh mushrooms or large cultivated mushrooms with brown tops

200 g (7 oz) boiled potatoes

1 onion

1 tbsp butter

150 g (5 oz) boiled ham

200 g (7 oz) mozzarella

salt

pepper

1/2 sprig of parsley

olive oil for spreading

Preparation time:
20 minutes
Cooking time:
5 minutes

Per serving
approx. 1231 kJ / 293 cal
22 g protein, 15 g fat,
11 g carbohydrates

1 Dry the mushrooms with a dry cloth. Cut out the stalks and chop finely.

2 Cut the potatoes into small cubes. Peel and dice the onions. Heat the butter and fry the diced onion in it for about 2 minutes. Also dice the boiled ham and the mozzarella. Mix all the diced ingredients and spice with salt and pepper.

3 Wash the parsley, dry it and chop finely. Then mix it together with the chopped mushroom stalks and stuffing.

4 Put the stuffing into the mushrooms and spread olive oil over them. Grill the mushrooms for about 5 minutes.

POULTRY MEDALLIONS WITH MANGO DIP

1 Wash and dry the poultry meat and cut it into large pieces. Then mince together with the peeled potatoes.

2 Mix the meat dough with the eggs and knead with the salt, pepper, lemon peel, chopped herbs, soy sauce, rice wine and cornflour.

3 Make flat medallions out of the dough and fry them on the grill for 5 minutes on each side.

4 Pour the poultry stock and the cream into a saucepan to make the dip.

5 Peel the halves of the mango and cut them into large cubes, add these to the poultry stock and cream mixture and let the whole thing boil down by one third. Then make a purée of this and put it through a strainer.

6 Spice the sauce with the curry powder and the vinegar. Fold in the whipped cream and serve the dip with the poultry medallions. Garnish the complete dish with herbs.

Tip
You can also use boiled rice instead of potatoes in the meat dough.

Serves 4

750 g (1 lb 10 oz) chicken or turkey breast fillet

100 g (3.5 oz) boiled potatoes

3 eggs

salt

pepper

peel from 1/2 untreated lemon

2 tbsp chopped herbs

2 tsp soy sauce

2 tsp rice wine

1 tsp cornflour

1/4 l (9 fl oz) poultry stock

1/4 l (9 fl oz) scream

1/2 mango

2 tsp curry powder

1 tbsp vinegar

2 tbsp whipped cream

herbs for garnishing

Preparation time:
30 minutes
Cooking time:
20 minutes

Per serving
approx. 2727 kJ / 623 cal
54 g protein, 29 g fat,
13 g carbohydrates

DELICIOUS GRILL, SKEWER AND HOT STONE RECIPES

Whether the gathering is large or small, grilling is a lot of fun and very sociable. It is a delightful, healthy, and very diverse method of cooking which is becoming ever more popular.

LAMB CHOPS WITH MINT SAUCE ON A HOT STONE

Serves 4

50 g (1.75 oz) mint leaves

1/4 l (9 fl oz) apple juice

1/4 l (9 fl oz) white wine

500 g (17 oz) icing sugar

green food colouring

4 double 160 g (5.5 oz) lamb chops

3 tbsp olive oil

1 tbsp curry powder

1 pinch of cinnamon

salt

pepper

mint for garnishing

Preparation time (without waiting time): 25 minutes
Cooking time: 30 minutes

Per serving approx. 5275 kJ / 1262 cal 23 g protein, 66 g fat, 133 g carbohydrates

1 Wash and dry the mint leaves. Keep some of the leaves aside, pour boiling water over the rest of them and let them soak while covered for about 1 hour.

2 Afterwards, pour into a strainer and catch the liquid.

3 Boil this liquid together with the apple juice, the white wine and the icing sugar for 10 minutes. Depending on your taste, you can make the mint sauce even greener with the food colouring.

4 Wash and dry the lamb chops. Mix the oil with the spices and spread it onto the lamb chops.

5 Grill the lamb chops for about 5 – 8 minutes on each side on the hot stone. Afterwards, serve the chops with the mint sauce, garnished with mint, and serve immediately.

RASNICI WITH RAW ONIONS

1 Wash and dry the meat and then cut into small narrow rectangles.

2 Sprinkle sugar on the meat, pour oil over it and mix everything together well.

3 Peel the shallots and cut them into fine cubes. Peel the clove of garlic and press it finely. Mix both of these with the soy sauce, the pepper and the flour. Pour the marinade over the meat pieces and let it marinate for about 30 minutes.

4 Afterwards, shake off the excess liquid from the pieces of meat and put them onto skewers. Grill the meat skewers for about 3 minutes on each side.

5 In the meantime, peel and coarsely chop the Spanish onion.

6 Sprinkle the skewers with the onion cubes and serve.

Serves 4

500 g (17 oz) beef fillet

2 tbsp sugar

2 tbsp oil

2 shallots

1 clove of garlic

4 tbsp soy sauce

pepper

1 tbsp flour

1 Spanish onion

Preparation time
(without marinating time):
25 minutes
Cooking time:
10 minutes

Per serving
approx. 1102 kJ / 264 cal
27 g protein, 12 g fat,
12 g carbohydrates

STUFFED TURKEY

Serves 4

2 turkey legs, 400 g (14 oz) each

salt

pepper

3 celery sticks

3 onions

2 apples

2 tbsp butter

2 tbsp soy sauce

2 tbsp honey

2 tbsp sherry

Preparation time:
30 minutes
Cooking time:
40 minutes

Per serving
approx. 1826 kJ / 437 cal
43 g protein, 14 g fat,
24 g carbohydrates

1 Wash and dry the meat well. Remove the bone and spice the meat with salt and pepper.

2 Wash the celery, remove the hard outer layers and cut into slices 1 cm (0.4 in) thick. Peel and dice the onions. Peel and quarter the apples, remove the core and cut the quarters into slices.

3 Heat the butter and stew the vegetables and fruits in until it is half-cooked. Spice the whole thing with salt and pepper and stuff it into the turkey. Then tie up the turkey with kitchen twine.

4 Mix the soy sauce together with the honey and the sherry and spread the mixture on the turkey. Let it dry a little and then grill the turkey for 35 – 45 minutes with frequent turning.

CALF'S LIVER, INDIAN STYLE ON A HOT STONE

1 Wash and dry the liver and cut it into 1 cm (0.4 in) thick slices.

2 Mix the sherry, the soy sauce and the curry powder and marinate the strips of liver in it for about 1 hour.

3 Peel the lemon completely, discarding all bits of the white skin. Then separate the lemon into wedges.

4 Place the mandarins onto a strainer and shake off the excess liquid.

5 Clean the spring onions, chop off about one third of the green part and then cut the remainder into quarters.

6 Remove the strips of liver from the marinade and shake off the excess liquid. Then fry on the hot stone for about 5 minutes with frequent turning.

7 Next put the lemon and pieces of mandarin together with the spring onions onto the hot stone and fry for about 4 minutes.

8 Salt the strips of liver and serve, garnished with sage, the fruit and spring onions.

Serves 4

500 g (17 oz) calf's liver

3 tbsp sherry

3 tbsp soy sauce

1 tbsp curry powder

1 lemon

1 small can of mandarins

1 bundle of spring onions

salt

sage for garnishing

Preparation time (without marinating time): 30 minutes
Cooking time: 10 minutes

Per serving approx. 977 kJ / 234 cal 26 g protein, 5 g fat, 16 g carbohydrates

GRILLED TROUT

Serves 4

80 g (2.75 oz) streaky bacon

1 tbsp mustard

1 bundle of chives

chervil

1 tbsp grated cheese

1 tbsp breadcrumbs

4 fresh, ready to cook trout

salt

lemon juice

pepper

herbs for garnishing

Preparation time:
25 minutes
Cooking time:
15 minutes

Per serving
approx. 1847 kJ / 442 cal
53 g protein, 21 g fat,
4 g carbohydrates

1 Dice the bacon and lay it out in a frying pan.

2 Add the mustard. Wash and dry the herbs. Cut the leek into small rolls, remove the leek leaves from the stalk. Mix together with the cheese and the breadcrumbs.

3 Wash and dry the trout, salt them inside and outside and sprinkle with lemon juice.

4 Sprinkle the trout with pepper. Stuff the mixture of mustard and bacon into the trout and secure with toothpicks.

5 Cut into the trout skin about 3 – 4 times on each side and cook on the grill for about 5 minutes alternating each side.

6 Garnish the grilled trout with herbs and serve.

GOURMET SKEWER OF KIDNEY

1 Cut the kidneys in half, clean them and remove the tendons. Soak them in water for about 30 minutes.

2 Then dry them carefully and rub in the lemon-pepper seasoning.

3 Wrap each piece of kidney with a slice of bacon and spice with paprika powder and the sage.

4 Peel and quarter the onions. Alternate the onion quarters with the kidney pieces on the skewer.

5 Sprinkle the skewers with Cognac and grill for about 6 minutes on each side.

Serves 4

6 veal kidneys

lemon-pepper seasoning

12 slices of bacon

paprika powder

1 tsp ground sage

4 onions

2 cl (scant 1 fl oz) Cognac

Preparation time
(without waiting time):
25 minutes
Cooking time:
15 minutes

Per serving
approx. 1303 kJ / 312 cal
26 g protein, 20 g fat,
3 g carbohydrates

55

SATÉ SKEWERS WITH PEANUT SAUCE

Serves 4

2 tbsp lemon juice

1 tbsp soy sauce

1/4 l (9 fl oz) coconut milk

1 tsp ground coriander seeds

1 onion

2 cloves of garlic

1 cm (0.4 in) ginger root

600 g (1 lb 5 oz) chicken breast fillet

2 shallots

2 red and/or green chilies

1 tbsp oil

1 tbsp ground ginger

150 g (5 oz) peanut butter

2 tbsp milk

Preparation time (without marinating time): 30 minutes
Cooking time: 20 minutes

Per serving approx. 2047 kJ / 487 cal
45 g protein, 23 g fat,
14 g carbohydrates

1 Mix the lemon juice with the soy sauce, the coconut milk and the ground coriander.

2 Peel the onion, the cloves of garlic and the ginger root, chop finely and fold into the mixture.

3 Cut the chicken breast into 1/2 cm (0.2 in) thick slices and let them soak in the marinade while covered for about 1 hour.

4 In the meantime, prepare the peanut sauce. First, peel and dice the shallots.

5 Wash and dice the chilies. Sauté lightly together with the shallot cubes in heated oil.

6 Add the ginger powder, fry this for a short time and then thin everything with the peanut butter, milk and 125 ml (4 fl oz) of water. Let it boil, spice with soy sauce and keep warm.

7 Then, take the chicken breast strips out of the marinade; thread them onto wooden skewers and cook on the grill for about 7 minutes on each side. Serve together with the peanut sauce.

BEEF SATÉ WITH PEANUT SAUCE

Cut 600 g (1 lb 5 oz) of beef into 3 x 10 cm (1.2 x 4 in) strips and let them soak in the marinade described in the basic recipe for about 1 hour. Cut 100 g (3.5 oz) of streaky bacon into long thin strips and then again into 3 x 10 cm (1.2 x 4 in) trips. Take the beef strips out of the marinade, put a strip of bacon on each one and then thread the strips onto wooden skewers. Cook on the grill for about 7 minutes on each side and serve with the peanut sauce.

Serves 4

Preparation time
(without marinating time):
30 minutes
Cooking time:
20 minutes

Per serving
approx. 2433 kJ / 582 cal
44 g protein, 41 g fat,
7 g carbohydrate

LAMB SATÉ WITH PEANUT SAUCE

Cut 600 g (1 lb 5 oz) of lamb into small cubes and let it marinade for about 1 hour in a marinade made of 3 tsp of freshly grated ginger, 4 tbsp of rice wine or sherry, 3 tbsp soy sauce, 3 tbsp sesame oil and 1/2 tsp ground coriander. Thread the pieces of lamb onto skewers and cook on the grill for about 7 minutes on each side and serve with the peanut sauce.

Serves 4

Preparation time
(without marinating time):
30 minutes
Cooking time:
20 minutes

Per serving
approx. 2713 kJ / 649 cal
48 g protein, 51 g fat
5 g carbohydrates

GRILLED LEG OF VEAL

Serves 4

**2 legs of veal,
1–1.2 kg
(2.2–2.6 lb) each**

4 tbsp honey

8 tbsp lemon juice

8 tbsp chili sauce

**1 tsp rosemary
needles**

salt

2 cloves of garlic

oil for spreading

Preparation time
(without marinating time):
20 minutes
Cooking time:
1 hour

Per serving
approx. 2289 kJ / 548 cal
75 g protein, 13 g fat
22 g carbohydrates

1 Wash and dry the legs of veal and place them onto a sufficiently large piece of aluminium foil.

2 Heat up the honey and mix with the lemon juice, chili sauce, rosemary needles and some salt.

3 Spread this thickly over the meat and then wrap up tightly in aluminium foil. Let the marinade soak in overnight.

4 Peel and cut the cloves of garlic in half. Unwrap the meat from the foil, shake off the excess liquid and stud with the halves of garlic.

5 Spread oil over the legs of veal and cook on the grill for about 1 hour with frequent turning.

ENTRECÔTE WITH GRILLED TOMATOES

1 Wash and dry the meat and spice with salt and pepper.

2 Wash the tomatoes, cut off the tops and scrape out the contents with a spoon.

3 Cut the mozzarella into small cubes, mix with the oil and herbs and stuff into the tomatoes.

4 Grill the entrecôtes for about 5 minutes on each side, grill the tomatoes for about 10 minutes.

5 Place a knob of herb butter onto the entrecôtes and serve with the tomatoes.

Serves 4

4 slices of entrecôte, 1–1.5 cm (0.4–0.6 in) thick

salt

pepper

4 large tomatoes

100 g (3.5 oz) mozzarella

2 tbsp olive oil

1 tsp herbes de Provence

60 g (2 oz) herb butter

Preparation time:
20 minutes
Cooking time:
15 minutes

Per serving
approx. 2325 kJ / 556 cal
59 g protein, 34 g fat
3 g carbohydrates

STUFFED PORK CHOPS

Serves 4

4 pork chops,
200 g (7 oz) each,
with pocket

200 g (7 oz) boiled
potatoes

200 g (7 oz) minced
onion

salt

pepper

paprika powder

2cl (scant 1 fl oz)
clear corn liquor

2 tbsp oil

1 tsp ground thyme

2 tsp ground
marjoram

1 onion

Preparation time:
25 minutes
Cooking time:
20 minutes

Per serving
approx. 2407 kJ / 576 cal
53 g protein, 34 g fat,
8 g carbohydrates

1 Wash and dry the chops.

2 Peel and dice the potatoes. Knead the potatoes with the minced onion and add salt, pepper, paprika powder and the corn liquor.

3 Stuff the chops with the mixture. Close the pockets with toothpicks.

4 Mix the oil with the herbs and spread it all over the chops. Grill for about 8 minutes on each side.

5 Peel and dice the onion and sprinkle it over the finished chops. Serve immediately.

LEGS OF CHICKEN WITH FRUIT

1 Wash and dry the chicken legs and rub the spices into them. Then cook on the grill for about 10 minutes on each side.

2 In the meantime separate the juice from the fruit, shake off the excess liquid and cut into cubes.

3 Briefly fry the fruit in butter, then thin down the mixture with the sherry and the stock. Let the whole thing boil down to half its volume.

4 Add the cream, let the mixture boil down again and add salt and curry powder.

5 Arrange the fruit on the chicken legs and serve garnished with the cocktail cherries.

Serves 4

4 chicken legs

salt

pepper

curry powder

1 pinch of cinnamon

3 halves of tinned peaches

4 slices of tinned pineapple

1 tbsp butter for frying

3 tbsp sherry

4 tbsp chicken stock

1 cup of sweet cream

cocktail cherries on a stick for garnishing

Preparation time:
15 minutes
Cooking time:
25 minutes

Per serving
approx. 2618 kJ / 626 cal
41 g protein, 42 g fat,
15 g carbohydrates

ROAST HAM WITH TRUFFLES

Serves 4

1 can of truffles
(40 g/1.5 oz)

500 g (17 oz) roast
ham with rind

1 onion

2 cloves of garlic

2 tbsp mustard

mixed garden
vegetables and herbs
(chives, parsley,
celery, chervils,
leek, lovage)

1 tsp pepper

1 tbsp honey

1 tbsp sugar

1 tbsp olive oil

1/4 l (9 fl oz) dark beer

1 pinch caraway
seeds

1 tsp ground
marjoram

Preparation time:
30 minutes
Cooking time:
1 hour

Per serving
approx. 1209 kJ / 288 cal
26 g protein, 11 g fat,
11 g carbohydrates

1 Pour the liquid off the truffles, shake off the excess liquid from them and cut into strips. Wash and dry the roast ham.

2 Make small holes in the ham with a sharp knife and push the truffle strips into these, and then cut square shapes into the rind.

3 Peel and dice the onion and the cloves of garlic. Then mix together the mustard, pepper, honey, sugar, oil, dark beer, caraway seeds and the marjoram.

4 Spread the mixture over the roast, fix it in the grill basket and cook for about 1 hour. While doing so, keep it basted with the marinade.

HERB SOLE ON THE HOT STONE

1 Wash and dry the fillets of sole and spice them with salt and pepper.

2 Wash and dry the chives and the parsley and chop them finely.

3 Peel the clove of garlic and press it together with some salt.

4 Using the butter at room temperature, mix the herbes de Provence, clove of garlic, chives and the parsley. Then add salt, pepper and lemon juice.

5 Lay out the fillets of sole on the worktop, spread with herb butter and roll them up securing the rolls with toothpicks. Grill the rolls on the hot stone for about 5 minutes on each side.

6 In the meantime, cut the bacon into strips and bake on the hot stone until crisp.

7 Arrange the rolls of sole and the strips of bacon and serve.

Serves 4

400 g (14 oz) sole fillets

salt

pepper

1 sprig of chives

1 sprig of parsley

1 clove of garlic

100 g (3.5 oz) butter

1 tsp herbes de Provence

1 tbsp lemon juice

100 g (3.5 oz) bacon

Preparation time:
20 minutes
Cooking time:
10 minutes

Per serving
approx. 1566 kJ / 373 cal
23 g protein, 27 g fat,
1 g carbohydrates

ROLLED PORK WITH HERBS

Serves 4

8 slices of fresh pork belly

1 zucchini

salt

pepper

1 tsp dried Italian herbs

2 tbsp balsamico vinegar

1/2 red pepper

1 onion

1 small chili

1/2 tsp potted peppercorns

3 tbsp olive oil

herbs for garnishing

Preparation time: 30 minutes
Cooking time: 20 minutes

Per serving approx. 2463 kJ / 589 cal
18 g protein, 52 g fat,
3 g carbohydrates

1 Wash and dry the pieces of meat. Then spread them out on the worktop.

2 Wash the zucchini and cut lengthways into slices. Lay the zucchini slices onto the slices of pork belly.

3 Spice the whole thing heavily with salt, pepper and the herbs. Roll up the meat and secure with toothpicks. Grill the rolls until they are brown and crisp.

4 For the sauce, pour the vinegar into a bowl. Wash and dice the red pepper. Then peel and dice the onion.

5 Clean the chili and cut it into strips. Add it to the vinegar together with the diced pepper and onion and the peppercorns. Slowly add the oil while constantly stirring. Serve the sauce with the herb belly rolls. Garnish with herbs.

FRUIT SAUCE

Soften 150 g (5 oz) of mixed dried fruit. Boil 1/4 l (9 fl oz) vegetable stock. Stir in and boil 1 packet of cream sauce (a ready to use product) and let it simmer for about 1 minute while stirring. Cut the fruit into small pieces and add it to the sauce. Serve the fruit sauce with the herb pork rolls.

Serves 4

Preparation time:
5 minutes
Cooking time:
5 minutes

Per serving
approx. 597 kJ / 43 cal
3 g protein, 3 g fat,
26 g carbohydrate

TOMATO SAUCE

Melt 20 g (scant 1 oz) of butter in a saucepan. Add 30 g (1 oz) of flour and make a roux by simply stirring the mixture. Then add 2 tbsp of tomato purée. Lightly sauté. Thin the whole thing down with 400 g (14 oz) of tomato purée and let it boil. Add salt, pepper and paprika powder to the sauce. Then let it completely cool down. Whisk 3 tbsp of apple sauce into the mixture shortly before serving.

Serves 4

Preparation time:
5 minutes
Cooking time
(without cooling time):
15 minutes

Per serving
approx. 427 kJ / 101 cal
2 g protein, 4 g fat,
11 g carbohydrates

MARINATED NECK STEAKS ON THE HOT STONE

Serves 4

2 tbsp lime juice

1/4 l (9 fl oz) orange juice

1/8 l (4.5 fl oz) olive oil

2 cloves of garlic

1 tbsp rock salt

1 tsp black pepper

2 bay leaves

4 pork neck steaks of 150 g (5 oz)

herbs for garnishing

Preparation time (without marinating time): 15 minutes
Cooking time: 15 minutes

Per serving approx. 2264 kJ / 539 cal 28 g protein, 39 g fat, 6 g carbohydrates

1 Mix together the lime juice, orange juice and the olive oil.

2 Peel and chop the cloves of garlic coarsely, then add these with salt and pepper to the juice and olive oil mixture.

3 Wash, dry and marinate the neck steaks. The steaks should be completely covered by the marinade. Let the meat soak in the marinade for at least 1 hour, or even better over night.

4 Take the steaks out of the marinade and cook on the hot stone for about 5 minutes on each side. Serve the steaks garnished with herbs.

JAPANESE FISH SKEWERS

1 Wash and dry the fish fillets, sprinkle with salt and lemon juice, then cut into 4 cm (1.6 in) cubes.

2 Mix the Sake with the oil, the soy sauce and the allspice powder. Put the cubes of fish into the marinade and let them soak in it for about 2 hours.

3 Thoroughly brush off the mussels under running water and remove the beard (byssus). Throw away any mussels, which are open.

4 Boil the mussels in salt water for about 5 minutes. Remove any mussels, which have not opened. Take out the mussel meat.

5 Cut the bacon into thin slices. Then cut the slices in half vertically. Wrap every mussel into a halved bacon slice.

6 Take the cubes of fish out of the marinade, shake off the excess liquid and thread them alternately with the mussels onto skewers. Cook in the electric grill for about 4 – 6 minutes.

Serves 4

1 kg (2 lb 3 oz) marine fish fillets (cod or pollack)

salt

lemon juice

100 ml (3 fl oz) Sake

100 ml (3 fl oz) oil

2 tbsp soy sauce

1 pinch of allspice powder

1 kg (2 lb 3 oz) mussels

100 g (3.5 oz) streaky bacon

Preparation time
(without marinating time):
30 minutes
Cooking time:
6 minutes

Per serving
approx. 2748 kJ / 658 cal
60 g protein, 38 g fat,
2 g carbohydrates

AMERICAN STYLE SPARERIBS

Serves 4

2 kg (4 lb 6 oz) spareribs

250 g (9 oz) tomato ketchup

150 g (5 oz) honey

2 tbsp oil

1/8 l (4.5 fl oz) pineapple juice

2 cloves of garlic

1 tbsp dried herbs

Preparation time (without marinating time): 15 minutes
Cooking time: 40 minutes

Per serving approx. 2445 kJ / 585 cal
40 g protein, 26 g fat, 43 g carbohydrates

1 Wash, dry and separate the ribs into portions.

2 Mix the ketchup with the honey, oil and pineapple juice.

3 Peel and press the cloves of garlic. Add these and the herbs to the marinade.

4 Let the ribs soak in the marinade for at least 30 minutes, even better overnight.

5 Take the ribs out of the marinade and grill for 35 – 45 minutes while turning frequently.

MEXICAN STYLE SPARERIBS

Let the ribs soak in a marinade made of 2 small chopped chilies, 6 tbsp oil, 3 diced tomatoes, 1 pinch of saffron, 2 chopped onions, 1 tsp mustard, 2 tsp Worcestershire sauce, salt and pepper for at least 30 minutes, even better overnight. Further cooking is as described in the base recipe.

PORTUGUESE STYLE SPARERIBS

Let the ribs soak in a marinade made of 3 tbsp white wine, 2 tbsp chopped, mixed herbs, 3 finely pressed cloves of garlic, 2 tbsp lemon juice, 1 tbsp mustard, 6 tbsp oil, 3 chopped anchovies, salt and pepper for at least 30 minutes, even better overnight. Further cooking is as described in the base recipe.

Serves 4

Preparation time
(without marinating time):
15 minutes
Cooking time:
40 minutes

Per serving
approx. 2215 kJ / 530 cal
40 g protein, 38 g fat,
3 g carbohydrates

Serves 4

Preparation time
(without marinating time):
15 minutes
Cooking time:
40 minutes

Per serving
approx. 2262 kJ / 541 cal
42 g protein, 39 g fat,
0 g carbohydrates

ALSACE STYLE STUFFED BREAST OF VEAL

Serves 4

1 kg (2 lb 3 oz) veal breast, with pocket

salt

pepper

paprika powder

4 tbsp sauerkraut

2 cl (scant 1 fl oz) dry white wine

100 g (3.5 oz) green grapes

2 eggs

1 cup of yoghurt

1 tbsp mustard

oil for spreading

Preparation time:
30 minutes
Cooking time:
50 minutes

Per serving
approx. 1923 kJ / 460 cal
52 g protein, 24 g fat,
7 g carbohydrates

1 Wash the meat, dry it and rub it with salt, pepper and paprika powder on the inside and outside.

2 Loosen the sauerkraut with a fork and mix it with the wine.

3 Peel the grapes, cut them into halves and remove the pips. Mix them together with the eggs, yoghurt and the mustard and fold in the sauerkraut. Add salt and pepper.

4 Fill the cavity with the sauerkraut mixture and tie it up with kitchen twine.

5 Spread oil over the breast of veal and wrap it in a sufficiently large piece of aluminium foil. Cook at an appropriate distance from the fire for about 35 minutes. Carefully remove the aluminium foil and cook the roast on the grill for a further 15 minutes on each side to make it really crispy. Carve the roast into slices and serve.

KING PRAWNS WITH AIOLI

1 Wash the king prawns, cut into the shell on the back and remove the offal. Hardboil 2 eggs for about 8 minutes.

2 Peel and dice the onion, and mix it together with the mustard powder, salt, peanut oil, lemon juice and the herbs to make a marinade.

3 Put the prawns into the marinade and let it soak there for about 2 hours.

4 Crumble the toast bread and purée with the milk and two raw eggs in a mixer.

5 Peel and dice the hardboiled eggs. Peel and press the garlic coarsely.

6 Put the diced eggs and the chopped garlic into the mixer as well and purée until creamy. Add the olive oil slowly while doing so. Spice the Aioli with salt, pepper, dill and mustard.

7 Take the king prawns out of the marinade, shake off the excess liquid and grill for 5 – 8 minutes. Serve the prawns with the Aioli.

Serves 4

1 kg (2 lb 3 oz) king prawns

4 eggs

1 onion

1 tsp mustard powder

1 tsp salt

1/8 l (4.5 fl oz) peanut oil

3 tbsp lemon juice

1 tbsp chopped herbs

100 g (3.5 oz) toast bread without the crust

1/8 l (4.5 fl oz) milk

8–10 cloves of garlic

1/2 l (17 fl oz) olive oil

salt

pepper

2 tbsp chopped dill

1 tbsp mustard

Preparation time (without marinating time): 30 minutes
Cooking time: 35 minutes

Per serving approx. 7104 kJ / 1719 cal 30 g protein, 166 g fat, 15 g carbohydrates

WILD BOAR MEDALLIONS WITH YELLOW BOLETUS

Serves 4

500 g (17 oz) wild boar fillet

salt

pepper

1 tsp ground thyme

1 tsp ground tarragon

150 g (5 oz) yellow boletus or brown mushrooms

8 slices of streaky bacon

2 oranges

2 tbsp Cognac

Preparation time:
20 minutes
Cooking time:
25 minutes

Per serving
approx. 1575 kJ / 377 cal
31 g protein, 22 g fat,
8 g carbohydrates

1 Wash and dry the fillets of wild boar and cut into 8 finger-thick medallions. Spice the medallions with salt, pepper, thyme and tarragon.

2 Dry the mushrooms with a dry cloth and cut into slices.

3 Lay the bacon out on the worktop. Place 2 mushroom slices on the centre of each slice of bacon. Place the medallions of wild boar on the mushrooms and then put 2 more slices of mushroom on top.

4 Wrap the bacon around the medallions and secure it with toothpicks.

5 Fry the medallions on the hot stone for 10 – 12 minutes with frequent turning.

6 Peel the oranges and cut into segments. Grill the orange segments on the hot stone for about 5 minutes, then put them into a small frying pan, sprinkle and flame with Cognac, and serve with the medallions of wild boar.

SALTIMBOCCA ON SKEWERS

1 Wash and dry the escalopes of pork and spice with salt, pepper and the herbs.

2 Lay out the escalopes on the worktop and place a slice of streaky bacon on each one.

3 Carefully rinse and dry the sage leaves. Put one sage leaf onto each slice of bacon.

4 Then sprinkle with the Parmesan and fold the escalopes together.

5 Thread 2 escalopes onto each skewer, spread olive oil over them and cook for about 10 minutes on each side.

6 Serve the saltimbocca garnished with basil and black olives.

Serves 4

8 thin escalopes
of pork,
100 g (3.5 oz) each

salt

pepper

1 tsp dried Italian
herbs

8 slices of streaky
bacon

8 sage leaves

3 tbsp grated
Parmesan cheese

2 tbsp olive oil

basil and black olives
for garnishing

Preparation time:
20 minutes
Cooking time:
20 minutes

Per serving
approx. 2396 kJ / 573 cal
52 g protein, 39 g fat,
0 g carbohydrates

ROAST BEEF WITH RED ONIONS

Serves 4

1 kg (2 lb 3 oz) roast beef

4 tbsp oil

3 tbsp mustard

1 tbsp salt

1 tsp cayenne pepper

2 cloves of garlic

1 tsp dried herbs (marjoram, parsley, rosemary, thyme)

4–6 red onions

2 tbsp butter

1 tube of store-bought remoulade sauce

Preparation time (without marinating time): 20 minutes
Cooking time: 40 minutes

Per serving approx. 4211 kJ / 1008 cal
53 g protein, 85 g fat,
3 g carbohydrates

1 Wash and dry the roast beef carefully.

2 Mix the oil, mustard, salt and the pepper. Peel and press the cloves of garlic finely. Add these and the dried herbs to the oil.

3 Spread marinade over the roast beef and let it soak in the marinade for at least 1 hour. It is even better overnight.

4 Take the meat out of the marinade, thread it onto a skewer and grill it directly over the fire for about 10 minutes. Then increase the distance away from the fire and grill it for another 20 minutes.

5 Peel and slice the onions. Grease a sufficiently large piece of aluminium foil with butter and put the onion rings onto it. Close the aluminium foil tightly and either cook the onions in the embers or on the grill for about 15 minutes.

6 Take the roast beef off the skewer and let it stand for about 10 minutes. Then carve it into slices and arrange it on the plate with the onions. Garnish with remoulade or add remoulade to it as a sauce.

GOURMET CHICKEN ON A HOT STONE

1 Wash and slice the aubergine.

2 Wash, dry and chop the chervil finely. Peel and dice the garlic. Mix both with the oil, lemon juice salt and pepper to make a marinade.

3 Put the slices of aubergine into the marinade and let them soak for about 1 hour.

4 Wash, dry and quarter the chicken breast fillets.

5 Mix the sherry with the ground ginger, salt, pepper and soy sauce and dip the chicken into the sauce on both sides.

6 Take the aubergine slices out of the marinade, shake off the excess liquid and cook them on the hot stone together with the pieces of chicken breast for about 3 – 4 minutes on each side. Arrange the pieces of chicken on the plate with the slices of aubergine and serve.

Serves 4

1 aubergine

2 sprigs of chervil

3 cloves of garlic

1/8 l (4.5 fl oz) olive oil

1 tbsp lemon juice

salt

pepper

4 chicken breast fillets

2 tbsp sherry

1 tsp ground ginger

1 tbsp soy sauce

Preparation time
(without marinating time):
30 minutes
Cooking time:
10 minutes

Per serving
approx. 1860 kJ / 445 cal
29 g protein, 32 g fat,
2 g carbohydrates

ROLLED ROAST TURKEY

Serves 4

750 g (1 lb 3 oz) turkey breast in one whole piece (prepared for a rolled roast)

salt

pepper

curry powder

4 tomatoes

1 bunch of spring onions

2 cloves of garlic

1 fennel

10 black olives

1 bunch of basil

2 sprigs of rosemary

1 egg

3 tbsp breadcrumbs

3 tbsp olive oil

1 tsp ground rosemary

Preparation time:
40 minutes
Cooking time:
1 hour

Per serving
approx. 1641 kJ / 390 cal
50 g protein, 12 g fat,
11 g carbohydrates

1 Wash and dry the meat, tap it reasonably flat between two sheets of plastic foil and lay it on the worktop. Spice the turkey breast with salt, pepper and curry powder.

2 Cut crosses in the tomatoes, pour boiling water over them, peel them, remove the seeds and cut them into cubes. Wash the spring onions and cut them into rings. Peel and finely press the cloves of garlic. Wash the fennel, remove the hard core and cut the fennel into strips. Finely chop the olives. Wash, dry and finely chop the herbs. Mix these ingredients together with the egg and the breadcrumbs.

3 Spread the mixture over the turkey breast, leaving a border of 2 cm (0.8 in). Then roll up the meat and tie it with kitchen twine.

4 Put the rolled roast onto a rotary spit and cook on the grill for about 1 hour. While cooking, turn frequently, baste with the oil several times and sprinkle with the rosemary.

5 After cooking, let the roast stand for a while, then carve into slices and serve.

GREEK STYLE ROLLED ROAST TURKEY

Here the rolled roast is filled with a stuffing made of 750 g (1 lb 10 oz) of blanched spinach, 1 chopped clove of garlic, 1 chopped onion, 50 g (1.75 oz) of green chopped olives, 200 g (7 oz) of cubed feta cheese, 1 egg and 3 tbsp of breadcrumbs. The dish is prepared the same way as the base recipe just mentioned.

Serves 4

Preparation time:
40 minutes
Cooking time:
1 hour

Per serving
approx. 2130 kJ / 510 cal
60 g protein, 22 g fat,
16 g carbohydrates

HUNGARIAN STYLE ROLLED ROAST TURKEY

In this variation, the rolled roast is stuffed with 500 g (17 oz) of red peppers cut into strips, 100 g (3.5 oz) of streaky bacon cut into cubes, 1 egg and 3 tbsp breadcrumbs. The stuffing is heavily spiced with salt, pepper and red paprika. Further cooking is done as described in the base recipe.

Serves 4

Preparation time:
20 minutes
Cooking time:
1 hour

Per serving
approx. 2145 kJ / 513 cal
54 g protein, 22 g fat,
19 g carbohydrates

LEG OF PORK WITH CUMIN

Serves 4

**4 legs of pork
(front legs,
200–250 g/7–9 oz
each)**

salt

pepper

2 tsp ground cumin

1/4 l (9 fl oz) beer

2 tbsp mustard

1 tsp marjoram

1 tsp thyme

1 tbsp oil

Preparation time:
10 minutes
Cooking time:
1 hour 10 minutes

Per serving
approx. 2077 kJ / 497 cal
28 g protein, 37 g fat,
3 g carbohydrates

1 Wash the legs of pork and put them into a sufficiently large saucepan of salt water. Bring the water to the boil and let the legs of pork simmer at medium heat for about 20 minutes.

2 Take the legs of pork out of the water, let them cool down a bit and dry them well.

3 Mix the spices with the beer, mustard, herbs and oil.

4 Spread the marinade over the legs of pork and cook on the grill for about 50 minutes. While cooking, baste them with the marinade and turn them frequently.

GOURMET MACKEREL

1 Wash and dry the mackerels, sprinkle with salt and lemon juice. Let them stand for about 10 minutes.

2 In the meantime cut crosses in the tomatoes, pour boiling water over them, then peel the tomatoes and remove the seeds. Cut into cubes.

3 Peel and dice the onions. Heat the oil and add the onions, followed by the diced tomato. Let everything braise for about 5 minutes.

4 Wash, dry and finely chop the herbs and add these to the mixture of tomatoes and onions. Stuff the mackerels with the mixture. Close and secure the belly opening with toothpicks. Cut into the mackerel skin 3 or 4 times on the sides.

5 Grill the mackerel for about 5 minutes on each side.

6 For the sauce, mix the yoghurt, sour cream and the almonds. Add salt and pepper and serve with the mackerel.

Serves 4

4 fresh, ready to cook mackerels

salt

lemon juice

4 tomatoes

2 onions

1 tbsp oil

1 bundle of dill, chives and chervils

2 cups of yoghurt

2 tbsp sour cream

2 tbsp chopped almonds

pepper

Preparation time:
25 minutes
Cooking time:
20 minutes

Per serving
approx. 3011 kJ / 720 cal
60 g protein, 45 g fat,
8 g carbohydrates

SOUTHERN STYLE CHICKEN SKEWERS

Serves 4

1/4 l (9 fl oz) yoghurt

2 tbsp olive oil

2 cloves of garlic

1/2 bundle of mint

pepper

500 g (17 oz) chicken breast fillets

100 g (3.5 oz) streaky bacon

2 onions

8 bay leaves

12 black olives without the stones

Preparation time (without marinating time): 30 minutes
Cooking time: 15 minutes

Per serving approx. 1520 kJ / 362 cal 36 g protein, 18 g fat, 4 g carbohydrates

1 Mix the yoghurt with the olive oil. Peel and finely press the cloves of garlic. Wash, dry and finely chop the mint. Fold the garlic and the mint into the yoghurt. Add pepper.

2 Wash, dry and cut the meat into large cubes. Put it into the yoghurt marinade and let it soak there for about 30 minutes.

3 Cut the streaky bacon into large strips. Peel and quarter the onions.

4 Take the cubes of meat out of the marinade, shake off the excess liquid and thread them alternately with the bacon, the onions, the bay leaves and the black olives onto skewers.

5 Cook the chicken skewers on the grill for about 5 – 8 minutes on each side.

ROAST BEEF "DIABOLO" (DEVILLED ROAST BEEF)

1 Wash, dry and divide the meat into servings.

2 Peel and dice the onions. Put these and the white wine into a saucepan and let it boil down by half.

3 Add the mustard and spice the sauce heavily with cayenne pepper and salt.

4 Spread the sauce over the pieces of meat and grill for about 4 minutes on each side. Serve garnished with herbs.

Serves 4

800 g (1.7 lb) prime rib of beef

2 onions

1/4 l (9 fl oz) white wine

2 tsp mustard

cayenne pepper

salt

herbs for garnishing

Preparation time:
20 minutes
Cooking time:
10 minutes

Per serving
approx. 2099 kJ / 502 cal
38 g protein, 33 g fat,
2 g carbohydrates

MIXED GRILL ON THE HOT STONE

Serves 4

200 g (7 oz) veal, beef, pork and turkey fillets

200 g (7 oz) streaky bacon

4 scampis

4 tbsp olive oil

salt

pepper

2 tsp dried, mixed herbs

2 tbsp lemon juice

1 mango

2 pears

1 small can of mandarin fillets (225 g/8 oz)

4 tomatoes

2 onions

200 g (7 oz) oyster mushrooms

2 cl (scant 1 fl oz) Williams pear spirit

Preparation time (without marinating time): 30 minutes
Cooking time: 15 minutes

Per serving approx. 2869 kJ / 687 cal 59 g protein, 35 g fat, 23 g carbohydrates

1 Wash and dry the meat well and cut it into 1 cm (0.4 in) slices.

2 First cut the bacon into slices and then into wide strips.

3 Clean the scampis, cut them lengthways and remove the offal.

4 Mix the oil with salt, pepper and herbs. Spread this over the meat and let the meat stand for about 20 minutes.

5 Marinate the scampis in the lemon juice for about 15 minutes.

6 Peel the mango and cut into pieces. Peel and cut the pears in half, remove the core and also cut into pieces. Strain the mandarin fillets and shake off the excess liquid.

7 Wash the tomatoes and cut them in halves. Peel the onions and cut them into slices approx. 1/2 cm (0.2 in) thick.

8 Wash the oyster mushrooms and cut them into large strips.

9 Sprinkle the pear spirit over the pieces of mango and pear.

10 Arrange all the ingredients on a plate and serve. Every guest can compose his own grill plate at the table and cook on the hot stone according to his taste.

FINE TURKEY ROLLS

1 Wash and dry the escalopes of turkey, tap them a bit flatter between two sheets of plastic foil and cut them in half lengthways. Spice the escalopes strongly with salt, pepper, coriander, and curry powder.

2 Peel and quarter the bananas. Put a banana quarter onto every escalope and roll it up. Secure the rolls with toothpicks cook on the grill for about 20 minutes with frequent turning.

3 Stir the yoghurt and the fresh cream into a smooth mixture and spice with salt, curry powder and pineapple juice.

4 Serve the turkey rolls together with the curry sauce.

Serves 4

4 thin turkey escalopes, 150 g (5 oz) each

salt

pepper

coriander powder

curry powder

2 bananas

1 cup of yoghurt

1 cup of fresh cream

2 tbsp pineapple juice

Preparation time: 25 minutes
Cooking time: 25 minutes

Per serving approx. 1572 kJ / 376 cal 39 g protein, 14 g fat, 18 g carbohydrates

AMERICAN STYLE LOBSTER

Serves 4

2 live lobsters, 1 kg (2 lb 3 oz) each or 2 frozen lobsters

300 g (10.6 oz) butter

salt

pepper

2 tsp paprika powder

1 lemon

watercress

Preparation time: 30 minutes
Cooking time: 20 minutes

Per serving approx. 3184 kJ / 758 cal 30 g protein, 65 g fat, 2 g carbohydrates

1 Put the lobster headfirst into boiling water and let it boil for about 4 minutes. People who do not like doing this can also use frozen lobsters.

2 Take the lobster out of the water, let it cool down a bit and cut it lengthways. Remove the bowels and the stomach.

3 Mix 60 g (2 oz) of the butter with salt, pepper and the paprika powder. Spread half of the spiced butter over the cut areas of the lobster.

4 Place the lobster onto the grill, first with the cut areas facing downwards and grill for about 6 minutes. Then turn the lobster halves over and spread these with the rest of the spiced butter and grill for another 10 minutes.

5 Cut the lemon into pieces. Melt the butter.

6 Garnish the lobster with the pieces of lemon and the watercress and serve with the melted butter.

ASIAN STYLE LEGS OF GOOSE

1 Wash the goose legs and pre-cook them in a pressure cooker with some salt water for about 20 – 30 minutes. Afterwards, take the goose legs out of the pressure cooker, let them cool down a bit and then dry them.

2 Mix the oil with salt and pepper and spread the mixture over the goose legs. Grill the legs on every side for about 15 – 20 minutes until the skin is crispy.

3 Shake off the excess liquid from the mushrooms and cut them into fine strips. Strain the bamboo shoots, shake off the excess liquid and also cut these into strips. Peel and dice the cloves of garlic.

4 Wash the spring onions and cut them into rings. Wash the chilies and cut these into strips.

5 Put the vegetables, sesame oil, soy sauce and the coriander leaves onto a sufficiently large piece of aluminium foil. Fold everything up in the foil and cook on the grill for about 15 minutes.

6 Serve the legs of goose together with the vegetables.

Serves 4

2 goose legs

salt

2 tbsp oil

pepper

6 dried, softened Chinese Morel mushrooms

200 g (7 oz) tinned bamboo shoots

2 cloves of garlic

3 spring onions

1 red chili

2 tsp sesame oil

2 tsp soy sauce

1/2 bunch of green coriander

Preparation time: 40 minutes
Cooking time: 40 minutes

Per serving approx. 1904 kJ / 453 cal 49 g protein, 24 g fat, 4 g carbohydrates

HALIBUT CUTLETS

Serves 4

1 onion

1 bunch of dill

1 bunch of chervils

4 tbsp oil

4 tbsp white wine

salt

pepper

4 halibut steaks,
250 g (9 oz) each

herbs and lemon
slices for garnishing

Preparation time
(without marinating time):
15 minutes
Cooking time:
10 minutes

Per serving
approx. 1646 kJ / 392 cal
50 g protein, 15 g fat,
1 g carbohydrates

1 Peel and dice the onion. Wash, dry and finely chop the herbs.

2 Mix the diced onions and the chopped herbs with the oil. Add the white wine, salt and pepper.

3 Wash and dry the fish cutlets and let them soak in the marinade for about 1 hour.

4 Take the fish cutlets out of the marinade; shake off the excess liquid and cook on the grill for about 4 minutes on each side.

5 Serve the halibut cutlets garnished with herbs and slices of lemon.

Tip

Surprise your family and guests with exotic types of fish such as swordfish or shark, which are sold as fish steaks.

HALIBUT CUTLETS WITH LEMON BUTTER

Wash the halibut steaks, spice them with salt and pepper and grill for about 4 minutes on each side. Melt 40 g (1.5 oz) of butter, take off the heat and mix with the juice of one lemon. Arrange the halibut cutlets on the plate; sprinkle them with shredded lemon peel and pour lemon butter over them. Garnish with dill and serve.

Serves 4

Preparation time:
10 minutes
Cooking time:
10 minutes

Per serving
approx. 1534 kJ / 365 cal
50 g protein, 14 g fat,
0.8 g carbohydrates

HALIBUT CUTLETS IN FOIL

Wash 4 halibut cutlets and spice them with salt. Grease 4 sufficiently large pieces of aluminium foil with 40 g (1.5 oz) of butter and place the halibut cutlets on it. Put 100 ml (3 fl oz) of vermouth (Martini), 4 tsp of coarsely ground white pepper, 1 bunch of chopped dill and the slices of one lemon into each "parcel". Close the aluminium foil and cook the "parcels" for about 15 minutes on the grill.

Serves 4

Preparation time:
15 minutes
Cooking time:
20 minutes

Per serving
approx. 1463 kJ / 350 cal
50 g protein, 14 g fat,
0 g carbohydrates

DOUBLE VENISON STEAK WITH WILD HERBS

Serves 4

800 g (1.7 lb) venison fillet

100 g (3.5 oz) mixed wild herbs (dandelion, bear's/wild garlic, sorrel)

1 box of cress

150 g (5 oz) grated cheese

4 slices of streaky bacon

2 tbsp oil

game spices

Preparation time: 20 minutes
Cooking time: 15 minutes

Per serving approx. 1894 kJ / 453 cal 54 g protein, 24 g fat, 1 g carbohydrates

1 Wash and dry the fillet of venison and cut it into 8 slices.

2 Wash, dry and finely chop the herbs. Mix the cheese with the herbs.

3 Lay out the venison fillets on the worktop. Distribute the mixture of cheese and herbs among 4 of the venison fillets.

Press the other 4 fillets on top. Wrap a slice of bacon around every double steak and bind it together with kitchen twine.

4 Spread oil over the venison steaks and grill for about 5 minutes on each side. After grilling, spice with the game spices and serve immediately.

PARMESAN FISH STEAKS

1 Wash the fish steaks and dry them with kitchen paper and then sprinkle them with lemon juice. Let the lemon juice soak in for a short time.

2 Sprinkle the mixed spices over the steaks.

3 Mix the Emmental and Parmesan cheese together and turn the steaks over in this mixture.

4 Cook the fish steaks on the grill for about 7 minutes on each side.

Serves 4

4 halibut or tuna steaks

1 lemon

Italian mixed spices (oregano, thyme, basil, bay leaf, sage, rosemary and garlic)

1 tbsp grated Parmesan cheese

1 tbsp grated Emmental cheese

Preparation time: 10 minutes
Cooking time: 15 minutes

Per serving approx. 1306 kJ / 313 cal 54 g protein, 8 g fat, 0 g carbohydrates

FANTASTIC DISHES FROM THE EMBERS

Childhood memories of camping,
hiking and a huge campfire are
easily rekindled with the flickering
of flames; and, when the wood
or coal turns to white ashes
you can start to barbecue.

HOT FRUIT SALAD IN FOIL

Serves 4

1 apple

1 pear

1 orange

1 grapefruit

3 tbsp lemon juice

2 tbsp brown (or demerara) sugar

2 tbsp rum

mint for garnishing

Preparation time:
20 minutes
Cooking time:
5 minutes

Per serving
approx. 514 kJ / 122 cal
1 g protein, 0.5 g fat,
22 g carbohydrates

1 Peel the apple and pear, remove the core and cut them into pieces.

2 Remove all the white skin from the orange and the grapefruit. Then cut out the wedges.

3 Mix the fruit with the lemon juice, sugar and rum.

4 Put the fruit salad onto 4 sufficiently large pieces of aluminium foil. Close the foil tightly and put the packages into the embers for 4 minutes. When cooked, take them out, arrange in the foil, decorate with mint and serve immediately.

VEGETABLES FROM THE FIRE

1 Wash the aubergine, remove the stalk and cut it in slices. Cut the slices of cheese in half and put 1/2 a slice of cheese between 2 slices of aubergine. Spice everything with salt and pepper and put 20g of the butter in flakes on top.

2 Wash and quarter the fennels, cut out the ends of the root and spice. Spread 20 g (scant 1 oz) of butter in flakes over them.

3 Next, wash the beef tomatoes, cut a cross in the top of them, spice and spread the cheese over them.

4 Shake off the excess liquid from the corn on the cob and dry them well. Melt the rest of the butter and spread it over the corn on the cob.

5 Spread out 4 sufficiently large pieces of aluminium foil on the worktop and put the vegetables onto them. Fold up the foil tightly.

6 Cook the vegetables in the embers for about 10 – 15 minutes.

Serves 4

1 aubergine

2 slices of Gouda cheese

salt

pepper

80 g (2.75 oz) butter

2 fennel bulbs

mixed spices (nutmeg, coriander, garlic, onion, bay leaf)

4 beef tomatoes

40 g (1.5 oz) Philadelphia cheese

fresh corn on the cob

Preparation time: 20 minutes
Cooking time: 15 minutes

Per serving approx. 1604 kJ / 384 cal 11 g protein, 24 g fat, 31 g carbohydrates

FILLETS OF HADDOCK WITH FENNEL

Serves 4

4 haddock,
150 g (5 oz) fillets

salt

lemon juice

2 spring onions

150 g (5 oz) cherry
tomatoes

2 fennel bulbs

pepper

oil for the
aluminium foil

dill for garnishing

Preparation time:
20 minutes
Cooking time:
20 minutes

Per serving
approx. 903 kJ / 215 cal
13 g protein, 3 g fat,
6 g carbohydrates

1 Wash and dry the fillets of haddock and spice them with salt. Sprinkle with lemon juice.

2 Wash the spring onions and cut them into rings. Wash the cherry tomatoes. Wash and slice the fennels. Mix the vegetables together and spice them with salt and pepper.

3 Grease 4 sufficiently large pieces of aluminium foil with oil. Put the vegetables on them and then put the fish on top of the vegetables. Close the aluminium foil tightly and put the packages into the embers.

4 Cook the fillets of haddock for about 15 minutes. After cooking, open the packages, arrange the fish on the vegetables, garnish with dill and serve.

LEG OF CHICKEN WITH HERBS

1 Wash and dry the chicken legs and spice them with salt, pepper and paprika powder.

2 Then wash, dry and finely chop the herbs. Peel and dice the clove of garlic and the onion.

3 Mix the oil with the herbs and the diced onion and garlic.

4 Spread the herb paste thickly over the chicken legs and wrap them into sufficiently large pieces of aluminium foil.

5 Put the packages into the embers and cook them for about 15 minutes. After cooking, remove the foil, arrange the chicken legs on the plates and serve.

Serves 4

8 chicken legs

salt

pepper

paprika powder

3 bunches of mixed herbs

1 onion

1 clove of garlic

4 tbsp oil

aluminium foil

Preparation time: 20 minutes
Cooking time: 15 minutes

Per serving approx. 3046 kJ / 728 cal 66 g protein, 50 g fat, 1 g carbohydrates

MARINATED LEG OF HARE

Serves 4

4 hare legs (frozen, approx. 1200 g/2.6 lb)

375 ml (13 fl oz) red wine

3 tbsp vinegar

1 bay leaf

5 peppercorns

salt

2 tbsp oil

2 onions

8 slices of streaky bacon

oil for the aluminium foil

4 sprigs of thyme

4 sprigs of marjoram

Preparation time (without marinating time): 30 minutes
Cooking time: 35 minutes

Per serving approx. 2545 kJ / 609 cal 70 g protein, 30 g fat, 2 g carbohydrates

1 Wash and dry the hare legs.

2 Mix the red wine with the vinegar, the bay leaf, the peppercorns, salt and oil. Marinate the hare legs in the mixture for about 12 hours.

3 Peel and slice the onions.

4 Spread out 4 sufficiently large pieces of aluminium foil on the worktop and grease them with oil. Take the hare legs out of the marinade and place them onto the aluminium foil. Cover the hare legs with the onions and 2 slices of bacon, 1 sprig of thyme and 1 sprig of marjoram on each. Close the aluminium foil tightly.

5 Cook the foil packages in the embers for about 25 – 35 minutes. Afterwards, open the packages, arrange the hare legs on the plates and serve.

BAKED HERRINGS

1 Wash and dry the herrings and spice them with salt and pepper.

2 Next wash, dry and finely chop the dill and the cress.

3 Peel and also finely chop the onions and the cloves of garlic.

4 Mix the olive oil with the herbs, the onions and the cloves of garlic. Spread the mixture over the fish and let it stand for a short time.

5 Grease 4 sufficiently large pieces of aluminium foil with some oil and place the herrings onto them.

6 Rub the lemon with a dry cloth and cut it into slices. Put one slice of lemon on each fish. Close the aluminium foil tightly.

7 Cook the packages in the embers for about 10 – 15 minutes. After cooking, arrange the herrings in the aluminium foil and serve.

Serves 4

4 ready to cook green herrings

salt

pepper

1 bunch of dill

1 box of cress

2 onions

2 cloves of garlic

3 tbsp olive oil

oil for the aluminium foil

1 untreated lemon

Preparation time:
20 minutes
Cooking time:
15 minutes

Per serving
approx. 2466 kJ / 590 cal
36 g protein, 44 g fat,
2 g carbohydrates

ZUCCHINI FROM THE FIRE

Serves 4

2 zucchini (courgettes)

2 onions

salt

pepper

150 g (5 oz) cooked ham

1 tbsp oil

Preparation time:
15 minutes
Cooking time:
10 minutes

Per serving
approx. 621 kJ / 148 cal
9 g protein, 10 g fat,
2 g carbohydrates

1 Wash and slice the zucchini. Peel the onions and cut them into rings. Mix the zucchini slices with the onion rings and spice with salt and pepper.

2 Cut the cooked ham into strips. Fold the strips of ham and the oil into the vegetables.

3 Put the vegetables onto 4 sufficiently large pieces of aluminium foil.

4 Close the aluminium foil. Put the vegetable packages into the embers and cook them there for about 10 minutes. After cooking, arrange and serve immediately.

STUFFED TOMATOES IN FOIL

1 Wash the tomatoes, cut off the top and scrape out the insides with a spoon. Put the tomatoes onto kitchen paper with the cut side facing downwards.

2 Dice the top and the pulp. Wash the spinach and shake off the excess liquid. Peel and dice the onion.

3 Heat the oil and glaze the diced onion in it. Add the spinach and steam for about 5 minutes.

4 Wash and dry the liver thoroughly and then dice it. Heat the butter and fry the diced liver in it for about 2 minutes while stirring constantly. Spice with salt and pepper afterwards.

5 Mix the diced tomatoes with the spinach, the liver, the breadcrumbs, the egg and the Parmesan cheese.

6 Stuff the mixture into the tomatoes and put them onto a sufficiently large piece of aluminium foil greased with oil. Fold the aluminium foil into a package and place it in the embers.

7 Grill the tomatoes for about 10 – 15 minutes, take them out of the foil, garnish with herbs and serve immediately.

Serves 4

8 beef tomatoes

500 g (17 oz) spinach

1 onion

1 tbsp oil

250 g (9 oz) poultry liver

1 tbsp gourmet butter

salt

pepper

3 tbsp breadcrumbs

1 egg

2 tbsp grated Parmesan cheese

oil for greasing

herbs for garnishing

Preparation time:
35 minutes
Cooking time:
15 minutes

Per serving
approx. 1418 kJ / 339 cal
28 g protein, 13 g fat,
23 g carbohydrates

SAUCES AND SIDE DISHES

A colourful collection of fine and spicy side dishes which enhance the wonderful smoky taste of the grillades. Our motto is: "everything that tastes good is allowed".

PINEAPPLE RELISH

Serves 4

250 g (9 oz) fresh pineapple

250 g (9 oz) fennel

1 onion

1/8 l (4.5 fl oz) vinegar

100 g (3.5 oz) sugar

1/2 bunch of dill

Preparation time:
20 minutes
Cooking time
(without cooling time):
15 minutes

Per serving
approx. 668 kJ / 159 cal
2 g protein, 0.3 g fat,
35 g carbohydrates

1 Peel and dice the pineapple. Wash the fennel and dice it as well, then peel and dice the onion.

2 Put the diced pineapple, fennel and onion into a saucepan together with the vinegar and the sugar and bring to the boil. Lower the temperature and let the relish simmer for about 10 minutes until it reaches the desired consistency.

3 Wash, dry and finely chop the dill and fold it into the relish. Let the relish cool down before serving.

MANGO RELISH

Peel 1 mango, remove the core and cut it into cubes. Peel and dice 1 shallot, and put this into a saucepan together with the diced mango, 4 tbsp of vinegar, 1 tsp of curry powder, salt, pepper and 2 tbsp of sugar. For cooking, follow instructions of the base recipe.

Serves 4

Preparation time:
15 minutes
Cooking time
(without cooling time):
15 minutes

Per serving
approx. 346 kJ / 82 cal
0.6 g protein, 0.1 g fat,
18 g carbohydrates

MELON RELISH

Dice the pulp of one small honey melon (250 g/9 oz) . Put this into a saucepan together with 2 diced onions, 1 diced chili, 50 g (1.75 oz) of raisins, 1/8 l (4.5 fl oz) of vinegar, 100 g (3.5 oz) of sugar, 1 tsp of curry powder and salt. For cooking, follow the instructions in the base recipe.

Serves 4

Preparation time:
15 minutes
Cooking time
(without cooling time):
15 minutes

Per serving
approx. 758 kJ / 180 cal
1 g protein, 1 g fat,
40 g carbohydrates

TARRAGON MAYONNAISE

Serves 4

3 egg yolks

1/2 tbsp salt

pepper

1 tbsp tarragon vinegar

1/2 l (17 fl oz) oil

1 tbsp capers

3 pickled gherkins

1 bunch of tarragon

Preparation time:
10 minutes
Cooking time:
10 minutes

Per serving
approx. 4990 kJ / 1194 cal
3 g protein, 130 g fat,
2 g carbohydrates

1 Whisk the egg yolks together with some salt and pepper. Slowly add the vinegar and keep whisking while doing so. Add the oil drop by drop to the egg yolk mixture and also keep whisking while doing so.

2 Shake off the excess liquid from the capers and the pickled gherkins and chop them finely.

3 Wash, dry and finely chop the tarragon.

4 Fold the capers, the pickled gherkins and the tarragon into the mayonnaise and salt and pepper to taste. Keep in a cold place until using.

PEARS, POACHED IN RED WINE

1 Peel the pears without cutting off the stalk.

2 Pour the wine into a saucepan and bring it to the boil together with the sugar, the pepper, the bay leaf and the lemon peel.

3 Put the pears into the wine and let the whole thing simmer for about 15 minutes while covered. Take the saucepan off the stove and let the pears in the decoction completely cool down.

4 Whip the cream, put a little sugar into it and then carefully fold the cranberries into the whipped cream.

5 Arrange the pears, garnish with the cranberries and serve as a side dish.

Serves 4

4 pears

1 bottle of red wine

3 tbsp sugar

1 tbsp black peppercorns

1 bay leaf

peel from 1 untreated lemon

1 cup of sweet cream

1 tbsp cranberries

Preparation time:
10 minutes
Cooking time
(without cooling time):
30 minutes

Per serving
approx. 1599 kJ / 382 cal
3 g protein, 16 g fat,
28 g carbohydrates

SPICY MUSHROOMS

Serves 4

juice of 1 lemon

20 g (scant 1 oz) salt

250 g (9 oz) white
mushrooms

250 g (9 oz) brown
mushrooms

2 tsp peppercorns

1 bay leaf

1 chili

1/2 l (17 fl oz)
brandy vinegar

40 g (1.5 oz) sugar

1 sprig of thyme

Preparation time:
10 minutes
Cooking time
(without cooling and
marinating time):
10 minutes

Per serving
approx. 350 kJ / 83 cal
3 g protein, 0.5 g fat,
12 g carbohydrates

1 Mix the lemon juice with salt and enough water. Wash the mushrooms in this.

2 Fill a large glass with the mushrooms.

3 Put the peppercorns into a saucepan together with the bay leaf, the chili, the vinegar and the sugar and bring to the boil.

4 Pour the brew onto the mushrooms. Lay the sprig of thyme on top and let the whole thing cool down. Then put a lid on the glass. Leave the mushrooms to soak in the glass for at least one night. Afterwards, take them out of the glass, arrange on plates and serve.

Tip

You can also use soft fruit aromas such as raspberry or grape with the mushrooms. Try the recipe with raspberry or cognac vinegar.

CUMBERLAND SAUCE

1 Wash and dry the lemon and orange, then chip the peel with a Julienne slicer. Squeeze the juice out of both fruits.

2 Boil the peel with a little water for a short time, then drain and shake off the excess liquid.

3 Peel and dice the shallots and slightly blanch them in boiling water. Then shake off the excess liquid.

4 Heat up the red currant jam in a water bath for a short time to liquify it. Let it cool down a little and fold in the fruit peel and the diced shallots.

5 Spice the sauce with the port wine, vinegar, orange and lemon juice, and add pepper, ginger and salt to taste.

Serves 4

1 untreated lemon

1 untreated orange

3 shallots

200 g (7 oz) red currant jam

3 tbsp port wine

1 tbsp vinegar

pepper

ginger

salt

Preparation time:
10 minutes
Cooking time:
15 minutes

Per serving
approx. 852 kJ / 204 cal
1 g protein, 0 g fat,
43 g carbohydrates

PAPRIKA AND CRESS BUTTER

Serves 4

250 g (9 oz) butter

1 box of cress

2 tsp lemon juice

salt

pepper

1 red pepper

1 pinch of cayenne pepper

paprika powder

2 tsp sherry

herbs for garnishing

Preparation time:
10 minutes
Cooking time
(without cooling time):
15 minutes

Per serving
approx. 2107 kJ / 501 cal
1 g protein, 51 g fat,
3 g carbohydrates

1 Whisk the butter and divide it into two halves. Wash and dry the cress and mix it with one half of the butter. Spice the cress butter with lemon juice, salt and pepper.

2 Wash and dice the paprika. Mix the diced paprika with the rest of the butter. Spice the paprika butter with salt, cayenne pepper, paprika powder and the sherry.

3 Fill a sufficiently large mould with a layer of cress butter. Let it harden in the fridge and put a layer of paprika butter on top of it afterwards. Let it cool and continue this procedure until all of the butter has been used. Then keep in a cool place until it is used.

4 Cut the paprika and cress butter into thick slices, garnish with herbs and serve.

HOME MADE MIXED PICKLES

1 Brush off the gherkins well under running water. Mix the salt with 1/2 l (17 fl oz) water and let the gherkins soak in it for 12 hours.

2 Wash the cauliflower and separate its flowers. Peel and slice the carrots. Wash the baby corn. Cut the pepper in half, wash it and then cut into 1 cm (0.4 in) strips.

3 Boil water in a sufficiently large saucepan. Blanch the vegetables in it for about 5 minutes, then take them out and dip them in iced water, then shake off the excess liquid.

4 Peel the onions. Take the gherkins out of the salt water and rinse them well.

5 Put the vegetables into a glass jar together with the bay leaves, the pepper, allspice and mustard seeds.

6 Boil the vinegar together with 3/8 l (13 fl oz) water and the sugar and pour it over the mixed pickles. Put a lid on the glass jar immediately and store in a cool place. After 3 – 4 days, drain off the liquid, boil it and pour over the mixed pickles again. The mixed pickles can be stored in a dark and cool place for 6 months.

Serves 4

250 g (9 oz) small gherkins

40 g (1.5 oz) salt

1/2 small cauliflower

125 g (4.5 oz) carrots

125 g (4.5 oz) baby corn

1 red pepper

100 g (3.5 oz) pearl onions (or pickling onions)

2 bay leaves

1 tsp black peppercorns

5 allspice (pimento) seeds

2 tsp mustard seeds

1/2 l (17 fl oz) vinegar

50 g (1.75 oz) sugar

Preparation time: 30 minutes
Cooking time (without standing time): 30 minutes

Per serving approx. 568 kJ / 136 cal 6 g protein, 1 g fat, 20 g carbohydrates

SAUCE HOLLANDAISE

Serves 4

250 g (9 oz) butter

3 egg yolks

salt

1 tbsp lemon juice

pepper

Preparation time:
5 minutes
Cooking time:
10 minutes

Per serving
approx. 2297 kJ / 547 cal
2 g protein, 55 g fat,
2 g carbohydrates

1 Slowly melt the butter. Meanwhile, whisk the egg yolks with some salt in a water bath.

2 Add the butter slowly while stirring. Spice the sauce with the lemon juice and pepper. Serve the sauce hollandaise immediately, as it cannot be kept warm or reheated.

SAUCE CHORON

Serves 4

Preparation time:
5 minutes
Cooking time:
10 minutes

Per serving
approx. 2322 kJ / 553 cal
2 g protein, 55 g fat,
3 g carbohydrates

For the sauce Choron prepare a sauce Béarnaise or Hollandaise based on the recipe described below and refine it with 2 – 3 tbsp of tomato purée.

SAUCE BÉARNAISE

1 Peel and dice the shallots. Wash, dry and finely chop the herbs.

2 Put the wine, the vinegar, the shallots and the herbs into a saucepan and boil the whole thing down to about 2 cl (scant 1 fl oz) of liquid. Then pass it through a fine strainer.

3 Slowly melt the butter. It must not become brown.

4 Whisk the egg yolks together with the herb liquid in a water bath. Slowly add the butter while stirring. Spice the sauce Béarnaise with salt and pepper and serve immediately.

Serves 4

2 shallots

1/2 bunch of tarragon

1/2 bunch of chervils

5 tbsp white wine

1 tbsp tarragon vinegar

150 g (5 oz) butter

3 egg yolks

pepper

salt

Preparation time:
10 minutes
Cooking time:
15 minutes

Per serving
approx. 1541 kJ / 367 cal
2 g protein, 35 g fat,
3 g carbohydrates

125

GOURMET MUSTARD DIP

Serves 4

150 g (5 oz) yellow mustard seeds

1/2 tbsp black peppercorns

1/2 tsp allspice (pimento) seeds

150 g (5 oz) brown sugar

200 ml (7 fl oz) wine vinegar

salt

1 bunch of mixed herbs

1 cup of yoghurt

1 pinch of ground cloves

1/2 tsp powdered ginger

Preparation time: 5 minutes
Cooking time (without cooling time): 15 minutes

Per serving approx. 1485 kJ / 353 cal 11 g protein, 11 g fat, 49 g carbohydrates

1 Grind the mustard seeds together with the peppercorns and the allspice seeds (medium fine). Mix with the brown sugar afterwards.

2 Boil the vinegar and slowly stir in the mixture. Spice the mixture with salt and let it cool down.

3 Wash, dry and finely chop the herbs. Stir the yoghurt until it is smooth and then fold it and the herbs into the mustard. Spice the dip with cloves and powdered ginger.

FIERY CHILI DIP

1 Peel and dice the onions and the cloves of garlic.

2 Cut the chilis in half, wash them and then cut into fine strips.

3 Heat the oil and glaze the onions in it for about 5 minutes. Add the garlic and the chili pepper and fry for another 3 minutes.

4 Add the vinegar, the sugar, the salt and the bay leaves and let the whole thing simmer at medium heat for about 20 minutes while covered.

5 Remove the bay leaves. Add the mustard powder and the tomato purée, fold these in carefully and then let everything cool down. Stir the cream cheese until it is smooth and fold it into the mixture.

Serves 4

125 g (4.5 oz) onions

2 cloves of garlic

2 chilis

3 tbsp oil

1/8 l (4.5 fl oz) brandy vinegar

25 g (1 oz) sugar

2 tsp salt

2 bay leaves

40 g (1.5 oz) mustard powder

2 tbsp tomato purée

250 g (9 oz) cream cheese

Preparation time:
15 minutes
Cooking time
(without cooling time):
40 minutes

Per serving
approx. 1622 kJ / 388 cal
9 g protein, 31 g fat,
11 g carbohydrates

MARINATED CHINESE VEGETABLES

Serves 4

1 red pepper

1 bunch of spring onions

300 g (10.6 oz) soya bean sprouts

1 small Chinese cabbage

2 cloves of garlic

1 piece of ginger root (2 cm/0.8 in)

1 tbsp brown sugar

2 tbsp vinegar

1 tsp Sambal Oelek

1 tbsp oil

2 tbsp soy sauce

green coriander for garnishing

Preparation time:
20 minutes
Cooking time
(without cooling and
marinating time):
15 minutes

Per serving
approx. 477 kJ / 113 cal
5 g protein, 3 g fat,
12 g carbohydrates

1 Cut the pepper in half, wash it and then cut into fine strips. Wash the spring onions and cut them into rings. Wash the soya bean sprouts and shake off the excess liquid. Wash the Chinese cabbage and cut it into strips. Put the vegetables into a sufficiently large bowl and mix them together.

2 Peel the cloves of garlic and the ginger. Dice both of them and boil together with the sugar, the vinegar, the Sambal Oelek, the oil and the soy sauce.

3 Let everything cool down and pour over the vegetables. Marinate the Chinese vegetables for at least one hour and then serve garnished with green coriander.

OLIVES AND CHEESE SAUCE

1 Shake off the excess liquid from the olives and dice them. Glaze them together with the chopped almonds in the heated oil for a short time. Dilute the whole thing with the white wine and boil it down to half its original volume.

2 Then add the vegetable stock, let it boil and spice with salt and pepper.

3 Mash the cream cheese with a fork and add it to the sauce. Take the sauce off the stove when the cheese has melted.

4 Wash and dry the herbs. Spice the sauce again with salt and pepper, garnish with herbs and serve warm.

Serves 4

60 g (2 oz) black olives without stones

1 tbsp chopped almonds

1 tbsp olive oil

1/8 l (4.5 fl oz) white wine

1/8 l (4.5 fl oz) vegetable stock (finished product)

salt

pepper

125 g (4.5 oz) cream cheese

1 sprig each of basil and thyme

Preparation time:
15 minutes
Cooking time:
20 minutes

Per serving
approx. 958 kJ / 229 cal
4 g protein, 20 g fat,
2 g carbohydrates

RUSSIAN STYLE SOUR VEGETABLES

Serves 4

250 g (9 oz) red beetroot

salt

250 g (9 oz) plums

250 g (9 oz) cooking apples

1/2 l (17 fl oz) apple juice

100 ml (3 fl oz) vinegar essence

100 g (3.5 oz) sugar

1 stick of cinnamon

1 tbsp allspice (pimento) seeds

1 tbsp coriander seeds

3 clove

Preparation time:
1 1/2 hours
Cooking time
(without cooling and
marinating time):
20 minutes

Per serving
approx. 995 kJ / 237 cal
1 g protein, 0.6 g fat,
53 g carbohydrates

1 Brush off the beetroot under running water for a short time and let it boil in salt water afterwards for about one and a half hours.

2 Quench the beetroot in cold water afterwards, peel it and cut it into pieces.

3 Peel the plums and remove the stones. Peel and quarter the apples, remove the cores and cut into slices.

4 Boil the apple juice together with the vinegar essence, the sugar, the cinnamon, the allspice seeds, the coriander seeds and the cloves.

5 Put the beetroot, the plums and the slices of apple into the apple vinegar and let the whole thing simmer at a mild heat for about 15 minutes.

6 Put the hot sour vegetables into screw-top glass jars, put the lids on and leave them there for at least 1 night.

APPLE AND HORSERADISH DIP

1 Peel and quarter the apples, remove the cores and put them together with the lemon juice, the meat stock, the cider and the sugar into a saucepan and let them boil until soft. Then purée the apples and let everything cool down.

2 Peel and finely grate the horseradish. Add the fresh cream and the horseradish to the apple sauce and stir everything together well. Spice the apple and horseradish dip with salt and serve.

Serves 4

2 apples

2 tsp lemon juice

1/8 l (4.5 fl oz) meat stock (finished product)

3 tbsp cider

2 tsp sugar

100 g (3.5 oz) horseradish

1 cup of fresh cream

salt

Preparation time:
5 minutes
Cooking time:
15 minutes

Per serving
approx. 752 kJ / 179 cal
2 g protein, 11 g fat,
13 g carbohydrates

SWEET AND SOUR CAULIFLOWER

Serves 4

1 medium size
cauliflower

salt

125 g (4.5 oz) sugar

2 onions

3 cloves of garlic

1 untreated lemon

2 star anis

2 dried chilis

1 tbsp peppercorns

3/8 l (13 fl oz)
vinegar

Preparation time:
15 minutes
Cooking time:
15 minutes

Per serving
approx. 846 kJ / 202 cal
6 g protein, 1 g fat,
39 g carbohydrates

1 Wash the cauliflower, separate its flowers and cook in boiling salt water for about 10 minutes. Then take it out, quench, let it cool down and put the flowers into a sufficiently large preserving jar.

2 Peel and finely chop the onions and the cloves of garlic. Rub the lemon with a dry cloth and cut it into slices. Distribute the onions, garlic and lemon together with the star anis, chilis and the peppercorns on the cauliflower.

3 Boil the vinegar together with 1/2 l (17 fl oz) water and the sugar and pour it over the cauliflower. Let the whole thing cool down and close the jar. Leave the cauliflower there for at least 12 hours.

132

ROQUEFORT BUTTER

1 Peel and finely chop the onions. Mash the Roquefort with a fork.

2 Put the room temperature butter into a bowl, add the onions and the Roquefort and mix thoroughly with a hand mixer.

3 Spice the Roquefort butter with the tarragon vinegar and some salt.

Serves 4

3 red onions

50 g (1.75 oz) Roquefort cheese

125 g (4.5 oz) butter

1 tsp tarragon vinegar

salt

Preparation time:
5 minutes
Cooking time:
10 minutes

Per serving
approx. 1265 kJ / 301 cal
3 g protein, 29 g fat,
2 g carbohydrates

HERB BUTTER

Serves 4

2 cloves of garlic

1 bunch of mixed herbs (basil, parsley, thyme, sage)

250 g (9 oz) butter

1 tbsp lemon juice

salt

pepper

Preparation time:
10 minutes
Cooking time
(without cooling time):
10 minutes

Per serving
approx. 2087 kJ / 497 cal
0.9 g protein, 51 g fat,
2 g carbohydrates

1 Peel the cloves of garlic and press them through a garlic press.

2 Wash, dry and finely chop the herbs.

3 Mix the garlic and the herbs with the room temperature butter.

4 Spice the herb butter with the lemon juice, salt and pepper. Then fill it into cups and put into the refrigerator to harden. To serve, put the cups into some hot water for a short time and squeeze the butter out.

GARLIC BUTTER

NUT BUTTER

Peel 6 cloves of garlic, mash them together with salt and fold them together with 1 small chopped green chili into 250 g (9 oz) butter. Spice the garlic butter with 1 tbsp soy sauce, salt and pepper. Fill the butter into an icing bag and squeeze out rosettes.

Chop 150 g (5 oz) of mixed nuts (hazel nuts, walnuts, pumpkin seeds, and sunflower seeds) and dry roast them without oil in a frying pan. Let them cool down and mix with 250 g (9 oz) butter, 1 tbsp of lemon juice, salt, pepper and 2 small chopped olives. Make the nut butter into a roll, leave it in a cool place and slice it with a crinkly knife.

Serves 4

Preparation time:
10 minutes
Cooking time
(without cooling time):
10 minutes

Per serving
approx. 2170 kJ / 516 cal
2 g protein, 52 g fat,
5 g carbohydrates

Serves 4

Preparation time:
10 minutes
Cooking time
(without cooling time):
10 minutes

Per serving
approx. 2913 kJ / 693 cal
7 g protein, 68 g fat,
7 g carbohydrates

SOUR BEANS

Serves 4

1/8 l (4.5 fl oz) white wine vinegar

2 onions

2 tbsp brown sugar

1 sprig of savory

salt

pepper

500 g (17 oz) young, green beans

herbs for garnishing

Preparation time:
15 minutes
Cooking time
(without cooling time):
25 minutes

Per serving
approx. 193 kJ / 46 cal
3 g protein, 0.2 g fat,
5 g carbohydrates

1 Boil the vinegar together with 1/8 l (4.5 fl oz) water.

2 Peel and dice the onions and put them into the boiling vinegar and water together with the sugar, the savory, salt and pepper.

3 Wash the beans and let them simmer in the brew for about 20 minutes.

4 Let the beans cool down in the brew, take them out, arrange them, garnish with herbs and serve.

SHALLOTS AND ORANGE DIP

1 Peel and dice the shallots. Heat the butter together with the oil and glaze the shallots in it. Spice with salt, sugar and pepper.

2 Mix the orange marmelade together with the liquor and orange juice and quench the shallots with the mixture. Let the whole thing simmer slightly for about 15 minutes while covered.

3 Afterwards, boil uncovered for approximately 5 minutes.

4 Wash the raisins, shake off the excess liquid and fold them together with the pine nuts into the dip.

5 Wash and dry the lemon balm and cut it into fine strips. Fold the lemon balm into the dip, arrange and serve.

Serves 4

250 g (9 oz) shallots

20 g (scant 1 oz) butter

1 tbsp oil

salt

sugar

pepper

1 tbsp orange marmelade

2 tbsp orange liquor

1/8 l (4.5 fl oz) orange juice

2 tbsp raisins

2 tbsp pine nuts

1 bunch of lemon balm

Preparation time: 15 minutes
Cooking time: 20 minutes

Per serving approx. 798 kJ / 190 cal 3 g protein, 9 g fat, 20 g carbohydrates

THANKSGIVING VEGETABLE POT

Serves 4

250 g (9 oz) gherkins

100 g (3.5 oz) pearl onions

2 each of green, red and yellow peppers

1 small cauliflower

salt

3/4 l (1.6 pt) brandy vinegar

350 g (12 oz) sugar

1 tsp grated horseradish

1 piece of ginger (2 cm/0.8 in)

2 bay leaves

3 cloves

1 tbsp mustard seeds

1 tbsp allspice (pimento) seeds

2 tbsp black peppercorns

herbs for garnishing

Preparation time:
20 minutes
Cooking time
(without marinating time):
25 minutes

Per serving
approx. 2351 kJ / 563 cal
9 g protein, 2 g fat,
112 g carbohydrates

1 Wash and dry the gherkins. Peel the onions, wash the peppers and cut it into pieces. Wash the cauliflower and separate its flowers.

2 Put the vegetables into a glass jar and sprinkle in layers with salt. Leave in the jar overnight.

3 Then wash the vegetables, dry them and put them in a glass jar again.

4 Put the vinegar, the sugar and the grated horseradish into a saucepan.

5 Peel the ginger, cut it into pieces and add it to the decoction together with the bay leaves, the cloves, the mustard and allspice seeds and the peppercorns. Let everything boil while stirring and pour it over the vegetables while hot.

6 Close the glass jar so that it is airtight and store in a cool place. Leave the vegetables there for 14 days. Garnish with herbs and serve.

SAUCE MALTAISE

1 Rub the blood orange well with a dry cloth. Cut the peel off in fine strips with a Julienne slicer. Mash out the orange. Melt the butter at a mild heat.

2 Whisk the egg yolks with 3 tbsp of the juice from the blood orange in a water bath. Fold in the butter slowly while stirring. Fold the strips of orange peel into the sauce.

3 Take the sauce off the stove, spice it with salt, pepper and Cointreau and serve immediately.

Serves 4
1 blood orange
250 g (9 oz) butter
3 egg yolks
salt
pepper
1 tbsp Cointreau

Preparation time:
10 minutes
Cooking time:
10 minutes

Per serving
approx. 2295 kJ / 547 cal
2 g protein, 55 g fat,
2 g carbohydrates

PICNIC AND BARBECUE

You can lighten up a grill party by giving it a theme. On the following pages, you will find a lot of imaginative ideas from the Bavarian bonfire to the huge American barbecue.

CREAMED HORSERADISH

Serves 8

2 cups of sweet cream

1 small stick of horseradish

salt

sugar

1 tbsp lemon juice

Preparation time:
10 minutes
Cooking time:
10 minutes

Per serving
approx. 1336 kJ / 320 cal
3 g protein, 19 g fat,
4 g carbohydrates

1 Pour the cream into a tall container and whip it.

2 Peel the horseradish and grate it. Fold the grated horseradish into the whipped cream and spice the whole thing with salt, a pinch of sugar and the lemon juice.

SAUERKRAUT WITH PINEAPPLE

Serves 8

3 onions

4 tbsp clarified butter (ghee)

1.5 kg (3.3 lb) sauerkraut

1/2 l (17 fl oz) white wine

pepper

2 tsp juniper berries

1 can of pineapple chunks (375 g/13 oz)

Preparation time:
15 minutes
Cooking time:
35 minutes

Per serving
approx. 581 kJ / 138 cal
3 g protein, 8 g fat,
10 g carbohydrates

1 Peel and dice the onions. Heat the clarified butter and glaze the onions in it.

2 Mix the sauerkraut with the onions, add the wine and the spices. Let the sauerkraut stew for about 30 minutes.

3 Put the pineapple chunks onto a strainer, drain and catch the juice. Mix the pineapple pieces with the sauerkraut.

4 Possibly spice the sauerkraut and pineapple mixture with some pineapple juice and serve.

SUCKLING PIG

> **Tip**
> *The champagne mustard (see recipe on page 138), the gourmet mustard dip (see recipe on page 126) and a bread circle are suitable side dishes.*

STUFFED SUCKLING PIG

Serves 4

1 suckling pig (6.75 kg
/15 lb carcass weight)

3/4 l (1.6 pt) lemon
juice

1/2 l (17 fl oz) orange
juice

1/4 l (9 fl oz) olive oil

2 tsp finely pressed
cloves of garlic

150 g (5 oz) coarse salt

2 tsp pepper

6 bay leaves

750 g (1 lb 10 oz)
sausage meat

4 onions

2 bunches of
mixed herbs

salt

paprika powder

**Please also see pages
16 and 17 for more
details.**

Preparation time
(without marinating time):
45 minutes
Cooking time: 3 hours

Per serving
approx. 1107 kJ / 739 cal
67 g protein, 44 g fat,
1 g carbohydrates

1 Wash and dry the suckling pig well.
Mix a marinade from the lemon juice,
orange juice, olive oil, cloves of garlic,
salt, pepper and bay leaves.

2 Rub the inside and the outside of the
pig with the marinade and then let it
stand for about 2 hours.

3 Put the sausage meat into a bowl.
Peel and dice the onions. Wash, dry
and finely chop the herbs. Knead everything together and spice with salt, pepper
and paprika powder.

4 Stuff the pig and sew it up with a
strong thread and put it onto a sufficiently large spit. Wrap the ears and legs
in aluminium foil.

5 Grill the pig for about 3 hours. Baste it
frequently with the marinade while
cooking. About 10 minutes before the end
of the cooking time, loosen the feet from
the spit and remove the aluminium foil.

MEAT SKEWERS WITH CHUTNEY

Serves 4

1 onion

1/8 l (4.5 fl oz) vinegar

100 g (3.5 oz) brown sugar

500 g (17 oz) lemon jelly

2 untreated lemons

cinnamon

cardamon powder

ground ginger

ground cloves

1 tbsp sherry

2 tsp salt

3 tbsp sugar

2 tbsp soy sauce

750 g (1 lb 10 oz) pork fillet

Preparation time:
40 minutes
Cooking time:
10 minutes

Per serving
approx. 2181 kJ / 519 cal
39 g protein, 13 g fat,
46 g carbohydrates

1 Peel and dice the onion. Let it simmer together with the vinegar and the sugar for about 10 minutes at a mild heat. Add the lemon jelly and let the whole thing boil to a syrup consistency.

2 Rub the lemons with a dry cloth. Slice off the peel with a Julienne slicer. Squeeze out the lemon juice. Stir the peel and the juice into the chutney and add the spices, then let it cool down.

3 Mix the sherry with the salt, the sugar and the soy sauce.

4 Wash and dry the pork fillet and cut it into thin slices. Thread the slices of meat onto skewers and spread marinade over them.

5 Cook the meat skewers on the grill for about 5 minutes on each side and serve with the lemon chutney.

CHICKEN WITH PINEAPPLE AND COCONUT

Serves 4

1 ready to cook chicken, approx. 900 g (2 lb)

salt

pepper

curry powder

1 can of pineapple pieces (125 g/4.5 oz)

2 tbsp lime juice

200 g (7 oz) coconut cream

200 g (7 oz) cream cheese

1 tsp chili paste

oil for spreading

Preparation time:
20 minutes
Cooking time:
1 hour, 20 minutes

Per serving
approx. 2133 kJ / 512 cal
38 g protein, 32 g fat,
9 g carbohydrates

1 Wash and dry the chicken well. Spice with salt, pepper and curry powder on the inside and the outside.

2 Put the pineapple pieces onto a strainer and shake off the excess liquid. Mix the pieces of fruit with the lime juice, the coconut cream, the cream cheese and the chili paste.

3 Stuff the chicken with the mixture and sew up the chicken tightly with kitchen twine.

4 Spread oil over the chicken and thread it onto a skewer. Grill the chicken filled with pineapple and coconut for about 1 hour and 20 minutes with frequent turning and basting.

SOUTHSEA BARBECUE

"PARADISE" FRUIT SALAD

Serves 4

2 coconuts

750 g (1 lb 10 oz) mixed fruit (melon, mango, pawpaw, kiwi, peach, carambola)

100 g (3.5 oz) sugar

4 tbsp white rum

Preparation time:
30 minutes
Cooking time:
10 minutes

Per serving
approx. 2323 kJ / 556 cal
7 g protein, 32 g fat,
57 g carbohydrates

1 Cut the coconuts in half and remove the coconut meat. Finely grate the coconut meat and sauté it without any fat in a frying pan until it is golden brown.

2 Wash and peel the fruit and cut into bite-sized pieces.

3 Mix the fruit with the sugar, the rum and the grated coconut and serve immediately.

FRICADELLES WITH MUSTARD

Serves 4

125 g (4.5 oz) beef shoulder

125 g (4.5 oz) pork shoulder

125 g (4.5 oz) veal shoulder

125 g (4.5 oz) fine sausage meat

1 onion

2 old baked, softened rolls

salt

pepper

nutmeg

mustard

Preparation time:
20 minutes
Cooking time:
15 minutes

Per serving
approx. 1163 kJ / 278 cal
27 g protein, 13 g fat,
12 g carbohydrates

1 Wash and dry the beef, pork and veal and mince in the mincer.

2 Afterwards knead the mince together with the sausage meat. Peel and dice the onion and add this to the mixture.

3 Press out the rolls well and add these to the mixture. Spice everything with salt, pepper and nutmeg.

4 Make fricadelles out of the mixture and cook these on the grill for about 6 minutes on each side. Serve afterwards with a lot of mustard.

GRILLED EEL

Serves 4

1 medium-sized eel

2 tbsp lemon juice

3 tbsp oil

1 tbsp vinegar

1 bay leaf

3 allspice seeds

1 tbsp chopped dill

1 tbsp chopped tarragon

salt

1 tsp peppercorns

Preparation time
(without marinating time):
20 minutes
Cooking time:
15 minutes

Per serving
approx. 2555 kJ / 611 cal
26 g protein, 53 g fat,
0 g carbohydrates

1 Wash the eel and cut it into pieces about 6 cm (2.4 in) long.

2 Mix the lemon juice with the oil, the vinegar, the bay leaf, the allspice seeds, the dill, tarragon, salt and the peppercorns.

3 Let the pieces of eel soak in the marinade for 2 – 3 hours. Then take them out, shake off the excess liquid and cook on the grill for 10 – 15 minutes. Turn frequently while cooking.

Tip
You can also serve Berlin cucumbers (see page 115) for your Spreewald country party. Rye rolls are also suitable.

PICKLED EGGS

Serves 4

150 g (5 oz) salt

2 bay leaves

10 peppercorns

10 coriander seeds

1 juniper berry

2 onions

8–10 eggs

Preparation time:
10 minutes
Cooking time
(without marinating time):
10 minutes

Per egg
approx. 403 kJ / 96 cal
7 g protein, 6 g fat,
0.3 g carbohydrates

1 Boil 1 1/2 l (1 qt 13 fl oz) of water with the salt, the bay leaves, the peppercorns, the coriander seeds and the juniper berry. Peel 1 onion (put the peelings on one side for later), cut it into rings and add it to the cooled down brine.

2 Hard-boil the eggs together with the onion peelings and the rest of the onion. Then quench the eggs and tap lightly on their shells. Add the eggs to the brine and let them soak in it for at least 24 hours.

3 Before eating them, spice the eggs either with salt, pepper and mustard, or vinegar and oil.

T-BONE STEAKS

GRILLED CORN ON THE COB

AMERICAN BARBECUE

Serves 4

4 T-Bone steaks,
250 g (9 oz) each

liquid garlic

1 tsp brown sugar

4 tbsp oil

pepper

salt

Preparation time:
5 minutes
Cooking time:
15 minutes

Per serving
approx. 1693 kJ / 405 cal
48 g protein, 23 g fat,
1 g carbohydrates

Serves 4

4 fresh or tinned
corncobs

salt

oil for spreading

pepper

50 g (1.75 oz) butter

2 tbsp green
peppercorns

whisky

Preparation time:
15 minutes
Cooking time:
15 minutes

Per serving
approx. 1217 kJ / 291 cal
4 g protein, 16 g fat,
33 g carbohydrates

1 Wash and dry the steaks well. Then rub them with the liquid garlic.

2 Sprinkle the sugar over the steaks and spread oil over them.

3 Grill the T-Bone steaks for about 5 – 6 minutes on each side. Spice with salt and pepper.

1 Wash or strain the corncobs, boil the fresh corncobs in slightly salted water for about 15 minutes, strain and dry them.

2 Spread oil over the corncobs and grill for about 10 minutes with frequent turning. Sprinkle them with salt and pepper after cooking.

3 Whisk the butter. Crush the peppercorns and fold them into the butter. Spice with some whisky and serve with the corncobs.

GRILLED CHICKEN WINGS

Serves 4

12 chicken wings

1 onion

2 cloves of garlic

1 chili

4 tbsp ketchup

salt

Preparation time
(without marinating time):
15 minutes
Cooking time:
10 minutes

Per serving
approx. 1642 kJ / 392 cal
40 g protein, 23 g fat,
5 g carbohydrates

1 Wash and dry the chicken wings well. Peel and dice the onion and the cloves of garlic.

2 Cut the chili in half, wash it and dice it as well. Mix the onion, the garlic and the chili with the ketchup.

3 Rub the mixture into the chicken wings and leave them to marinate for about 1 hour.

4 Then take the wings out of the marinade and grill for about 10 minutes with frequent turning. After cooking, sprinkle them with salt and serve.

BAKED POTATOES

Serves 4

8 potatoes
of 150 g (5 oz) each

2 tbsp oil

1 tsp paprika
powder

1 red chili

150 g (5 oz) cream
cheese

100 g (3.5 oz) sweet
cream

1/2 tsp mustard

3 tbsp lemon juice

salt

150 g (5 oz) bacon

Preparation time:
15 minutes
Cooking time:
1 hour

Per serving
approx. 2410 kJ / 574 cal
20 g protein, 25 g fat,
56 g carbohydrates

1 Brush off the potatoes under running water.

2 Mix the oil with the paprika powder. Grease 8 sufficiently large pieces of parchment with the spiced oil. Wrap up each potato in a sheet of parchment and tie up securely with kitchen twine. Bake the potatoes in the oven on the middle rack position at 200 °C/390 °F for about 1 hour.

3 Cut the chili in half, wash and dice it. Then stir it into a sauce with cream cheese, 100 ml (3 fl oz) water, the cream, the mustard, the lemon juice and salt.

4 First cut the bacon into slices and then into strips and cook in a frying pan. Fold into the sauce and serve with the potatoes.

Tip
Ready-made barbecue sauces and various types of ketchup also go well with American barbecues.

SAUSAGE SALAD

Serves 4

8 thick bockwurst
sausages

3 tbsp oil

4 tbsp vinegar

salt

pepper

sugar

1 onion

Preparation time
(without marinating time):
15 minutes
Cooking time:
10 minutes

Per serving
approx. 3097 kJ / 741 cal
28 g protein, 66 g fat,
1 g carbohydrates

1 Peel the sausages and cut them into thin strips afterwards.

2 Mix the oil with the vinegar and spice with the salt, pepper and some sugar.

3 Mix the salad sauce with the strips of sausage and let everything stand for about 30 minutes.

4 Peel the onion and cut it into rings. Arrange the salad, put the onion rings on top and serve.

GRILLED BLOOD SAUSAGE

Serves 4

oil for spreading

**600 g (1 lb 5 oz)
blood sausage**

2 onions

2 apples

4 slices of rye bread

grated marjoram

Preparation time:
10 minutes
Cooking time:
10 minutes

Per serving
approx. 1757 kJ / 418 cal
28 g protein, 26 g fat,
9 g carbohydrates

1 Spread oil on the grill rack. Cut the sausage into thick slices and cook on the grill for about 3 minutes on each side.

2 Peel the onions and cut them into rings. Peel the apples, remove the core and cut the apple into slices. Grill the slices of apple for about 2 – 4 minutes on each side.

3 Sprinkle the sausage and bread with marjoram and arrange together with the slices of apple and the onion rings.

RUSTIC PICNIC

CHEESE WITH ONION AND CUMIN

Serves 4

400 g (14 oz) Limburger cheese

8 tbsp vinegar

4 tbsp oil

3 onions

cumin

salt

pepper

Preparation time:
15 minutes
Cooking time:
5 minutes

Per serving
approx. 1573 kJ / 376 cal
52 g protein, 13 g fat,
2 g carbohydrates

1 Cut the Limburger cheese in slices and put it onto plates.

2 Stir the vinegar together with 1 tbsp water and the oil. Peel and dice the onions. Add them to the vinegar and oil marinade and spice the whole thing with cumin and salt.

3 Pour the marinade over the low-fat cheese and sprinkle with pepper.

Tip

Caraway and poppy seeds, and various types of bread and rolls also go well with a rustic picnic.